For my wife Harriett,

who has co-endured many disillusionments with the Church;

for our children and their spouses —

Karen, Steven, Terence, and Andrea;

but especially for our grandchildren —

Catherine and Elizabeth;

that one day they may see the Church restored.

O gracious Father, we humbly beseech thee for thy holy Catholic Church; that thou wouldest be pleased to fill it with all truth, in all peace. Where it is corrupt, purify it; where it is in error, direct it; where in any thing it is amiss, reform it. Where it is right, establish it; where it is in want, provide for it; where it is divided, reunite it; for the sake of him who died and rose again, and ever liveth to make intercession for us, Jesus Christ, thy Son, our Lord. *Amen.*

Book of Common Prayer, 1928

The Plight of the Church Traditionalist:

A Last Apology

ACKNOWLEDGMENTS

I should like to acknowledge with gratitude the support of The Prayer Book Society of the Episcopal Church. Without the encouragement of the Rev. Jerome F. Politzer, President, the Rt. Rev. Clarence R. Haden, S.T.D., D.D., Patron, and Mr. John Ott, Executive Director, this book would not have been possible. In addition to Fr. Politzer and Bp. Haden, the Rev. Dr. Gordon Griffith, the Rev. John Hildebrand, and my recently deceased friend and writing partner of many years, Dr. Lothar Kahn, read the manuscript and offered many valuable suggestions. I will always be grateful to Dr. Janet E. Hildebrand, who served as copyeditor, for her careful reading. Her many gratuitous marginal comments revealed the depth of her knowledge of the Episcopal Church, the wisdom of her evaluations, and the intensity of her devotion to the Christian religion.

D.D.H.

An Overview

To whom shall we look for leadership to lead the Episcopal Church out of the doctrinal and moral morass in which we are mired? We have every reason to look to our bishops for such a role. They bear apostolic responsibility and authority. For the past several decades, however, they have failed the Church miserably. Instead of believing in the historic faith they promised to defend, they are influenced by every vain doctrine that comes on the contemporary scene. They will not take an unpopular stand on any given question. The Spong fiasco in ordaining a practicing homosexual to the priesthood, thereby violating the expressed will of the Episcopal Church, is but further evidence of the breakdown of theology as well as simple morality among the bishops.

How about our priests? Are they not susceptible to a desire to stay in favor with their bishops? — an understandable though not a laudable attitude. They are protective of their "careers" and want to "get ahead," whatever that means. Instead of vocation we hear much about "my" ministry; they seemingly are not aware that the only ministry each of us has is derived from and authorized by our Lord Jesus Christ and is to be consonant, not with the culture of the day, but with His life and teaching. Our clergy are not as a whole equipped by education or commitment for the role of leadership that may well lead to a cross. Our seminary faculties, mostly erudite priests, must assume much of the responsibility for this condition. Thank God for those priests who are trying to teach and follow the orthodox faith despite all influences to turn them aside from their true vocation to serve the Lord in ways He approves.

Now we turn to the laity, 99% of the Church's membership. They have erroneously assumed that the work of the Church is chiefly the responsibility of the clergy. The clergy accept this concept, for it gives them an unwarranted prestige. There is also a latent, if not overt, refusal by the laity to get involved in religious concerns. This apathy is evident in the inability of the Church to get more than a relative handful of its members to participate in serious study of Prayer Book revision, ordination of women, human sexuality, ecumenism, or the Bible. Notable exceptions are not numerous enough to be significant, but we are hopeful that the laity will become increasingly aware of their role.

The word "doctrine" turns Episcopalians off as quickly as "evangelism," though this is the "decade of evangelism" in ECUSA. After all, according to the laity, it's the work of the clergy to deal with such matters as belief and getting new members. They are full-time and are paid salaries, aren't they? Isn't religion a personal matter, and wouldn't it be presumptuous for a lay person to inquire about what another believes or whether he/she goes to church?

The lack of lay involvement is resulting in further attempts by the present "liberal" hierarchy to water down the doctrine of the Episcopal Church even more! This is clearly seen in the new Supplemental Texts, Prayer Book Studies 30, an attempt to substitute feminist liberation theology for traditional orthodox theology. Though it was sent to a few carefully selected parishes and the seminaries, so inadequate — even heretical — is it, that one seminary, after study by faculty and students, has refused to use it, and another seminary has used it, only to become firmly convinced of its false inclusivity. In its report to the Standing Liturgical Commission (with copies to the bishops), faculty and students of this latter seminary point out its many failures to present the historic faith. God, Jesus Christ, sin are presented in such terms that only a pantheist would be comfortable with them. According to this latest liturgical presentation, God made all things and all people good; since He is a loving Creator all we have to do is praise Him. This bland, pedestrian liturgy and secular theology is but the newest attempt liturgically of the present liberal leadership of ECUSA to dilute the faith to the low level irreligious people want.

Another attempt to destroy the Episcopal Church is evident in the article beginning on the back page of the July, 1990, issue of *Episcopal Life*, the latest name of our national publication. It is introduced with the blurb, "The ecumenical giant is overcoming criticism and rising to new life." Most people thought the World Council of Churches was awaiting only a requiem, but here it is, holding a conference on "Peace, Justice and the Integrity of Creation." It is also significant that one of its leaders was Barbara Harris, the first woman Episcopal bishop, despite any qualifications other than that she has no adequate theological training, is of a minority group, and is a radical liberal. The ordination of women deacons has had its inevitable result — the consecration of a woman bishop, something the 1988 Lambeth Conference asked provinces to hold in abeyance until the mind of all provinces of the Anglican Communion could be ascertained. Impatient, arrogant ECUSA denied any collegiality of Anglican bishops by taking unilateral action in ordaining a woman of meager qualification to the episcopate. New Zealand quickly followed the American example in consecrating a woman bishop without waiting for the Anglican Provinces to reach a common mind on this problem.

COCU is not dead either. Liberals are reviving the subject of merging the Episcopal Church into a Protestant conglomeration in which the Episcopal Church would lose that which it has to contribute to a Protestantism which abandoned long ago the Catholic beginnings of Christianity. They have allowed COCU, because of its inherent fallacies and very weak support, to lie fallow for several years. Feeling the time is now ripe for the final blow to be given to our historic Episcopal heritage, the liberals are slipping it back into the mainstream of their agenda.

A prompt solution to these important and pressing problems is vital to our survival as a church of biblically based historic theology. The hope of our day is for the laity to become informed and involved in recapturing that which is essential to turning the tide of secularism and false liberalism. The laity are called upon by current events to rouse themselves from inertia and become committed to restoring the church to its former glory and purpose — the salvation of all mankind.

Dr. Hook has dealt most helpfully with these and other basic subjects in a scholarly, objective, realistic and fair way in this book, *The Plight of the Church Traditionalist: A Last Apology*. It is a must for everyone, laity and clergy, who wants to know what to do in these turbulent, chaotic times. I recommend that it be read by every traditionalist and that it be the basis of programs in every chapter and group meeting of traditionalists of whatever allegiance in the immediate days ahead.

The Rt. Rev. Clarence R. Haden, S.T.D., D.D.
Bishop of Northern California, Ret.
Patron
Episcopal Prayer Book Society

FOREWORD

I remember now, nearly six decades later, how as a four- or five-year-old I used to run to greet my father upon his return from an out-of-town business trip and ask what he had brought me. Once he brought me a truly marvelous present, a philosophical statement carved on a bar of steatite which read: "Hear no evil, see no evil, speak no evil," surmounted by three monkeys, one with his fingers in his ears, one with his hands over his eyes, and one with his hands over his mouth. Growing up, I puzzled over the statue many times because I was not sure whether the little figures were meant to convey the notion that it is bad to be a dispenser of evil, that evil will go away if ignored, or that the loss of one sense will dull the others.

Today, when I think of the monkey statue, I think of the Episcopal Church. Parishioners do not speak up about the mischief that is afoot in the church; the parochial clergy apparently see nothing unacceptable in their bishops' actions; and, the hierarchy refuses to hear complaints from below. The Church as a whole is like a person hunkered down in a corner, facing the walls, eyes tightly closed, with his fingers in his ears, and his lips pressed together in a hard line. You cannot talk to a person like this; you can only talk *about* him.

Let's begin to talk.

The Episcopal Church has become narrowly liberal-American, caught up in the frenzy of this country's social movements of every description. It no longer seeks primarily to serve the spiritual needs of its national membership, let alone to promote unity within the worldwide Anglican Communion. Instead, it fosters a multitude of national programs directed at everything from the liberation of women and homosexuals to the liberation of certain Latin American countries from the dreaded heavy hand of "dictators" backed by the U.S. The Church's function has changed from that of pastoral concern to social manipulation and political involvement. As the Rt. Rev. Robert C. Harvey makes clear in his *A House Divided*, this is not exactly a new phenomenon. On May 22, 1970, the Executive Council of the Episcopal Church passed a resolution demanding "[1] the immediate withdrawal of all U.S. armed forces from Southeast Asia, [2] a drastic reduction of strategic forces elsewhere in the world, and [3] [cessation] of the government's harassment of Black Panthers and use of National Guard and police in killing students."[1] In addition, the Council expressed its "support of striking and rioting students and called for a voluntary church offering to finance future strikes and to enable students to engage in 'political education campaigns' directed at their elders."[2] Hundreds of parishes throughout the United States communicated their dissatisfaction to the national church, but they were ignored. Ironically, the concerns of these churchmen were heeded only after a threatening letter from the Internal Revenue Service arrived at national church headquarters in New York City. Bishop Harvey reports that the Presiding Bishop, the Most Rev. John E. Hines, dispatched to all clergy a postcard which read: "Plans for a proposed offering on the 3rd Sunday in September 'for the support of student strike activities, including their political education campaigns,' have been suspended pending further action by the Executive Council at its meeting in October. ...The Internal Revenue Service has advised that implementation of the offering will jeopardize the tax-exempt status of the Domestic and Foreign Missionary Society."[3]

Is it the Church's mission to try to change society and influence foreign policy by the power of its organization and the use of its people's money without their consent?

Does such action violate the doctrine of separation of church and state?

Is it the place of any organization—particularly a religious organization—to assume only an imagined "liberal" stance on issues when, in fact, such a viewpoint may represent the position of less than the majority of the people? May one not legitimately object to a church's political or social involvement per se—and, even more, when that involvement is monolithically liberal?

What is wrong with examining every issue on its merits, treating some "liberally" and others "conservatively"? Common sense alone would seem to dictate that procedure.

It is, I think, not a question for me to answer but for the Church to explain, especially when one considers that the Episcopal Church used to be willing to accept members of diverse persuasion on a whole raft of matters. Ever since the Reformation, the denomination has dubbed itself "Catholic, evangelical, and reformed." Surely, such a tripartite arrangement has within it the seeds, if not the sprouts, of both liberalism and conservatism.

Not so long ago people used to designate Anglicanism half jocularly as liturgically "high and crazy, low and lazy, or broad and hazy"—with all the implications such a designation had for doctrine. However, these three relatively disparate factions managed to live together in harmony, thanks to the unifying force of the 1928 Prayer Book, a similar respect for Holy Scripture, and a healthy regard for received tradition based upon the Chicago-Lambeth Quadrilateral. Now the broadness (new translation: sociological concerns) has extended even beyond the denomination to include bodies of exceedingly hazy doctrine. To be sure, there is less high and low to contend with, but there is plenty that is crazy. Laziness may still be in evidence in some liturgical expression, but the vice is otherwise out of style. Fervor is the word to describe the liberals' efforts to level the Church both figuratively and literally. Former editor of *Punch*, that often iconoclastic, mordant journalist, Malcolm Muggeridge, indicts liberalism for the "darkness of our civilization" and describes it in his essay, "The Great Liberal Death Wish," from the collection of his pieces entitled *Things Past*, as "a solvent rather than a precipitate, a sedative rather than a stimulant, a slough rather than a precipice; blurring the edges of truth, the definition of virtue, the shape of beauty; a cracked bell, a mist, a death wish."[4]

What *is* a church liberal? How does one recognize him (or her)? He is a person without regard for the past, one locked onto an ever-changing present, a chameleon taking on the color of every new social movement, of every claim of every minority voice. He is suspicious of "abiding truths," eager to discover first-hand "truth" for himself — an individual's individual.

Yet, even such people cannot escape a certain conservatism, for in their rejection of tradition they band together as condensing fog. There are times, too, when, like free neutrons, as in nuclear fission, they interact strongly with nuclei, are readily absorbed, and decay into protons, electrons, and neutrinos with a half-life of c. 12 minutes. It is as hard to get hold of a liberal and his ideas as it is to grasp a neutron — and just as dangerous. Such notions may help to explain why the now thoroughly liberal Episcopal Church has become anti-sacramental. A sacrament is a sign or symbol of a deeper reality, an object or act of both form and substance, a means of grace — in short, something very real, very solid, and rooted in the historic Church from its inception. A sacrament is a mystery that can be grasped, literally and figuratively, an efficacious sign at which faith and action converge. Only the High Church faction has always felt comfortable with all seven sacraments. Now that haziness is everywhere in evidence, it is easy to imagine that all but Baptism and the Eucharist will evanesce — and even they are likely to undergo drastic changes. Besides, such a trend puts the Church more clearly in line with the Protestant bodies, who have never accepted more than two sacraments.

In 1973 the first serious resistance to the Church's changing character was undertaken. The Fellowship of Concerned Churchmen was formed, as they say, "as a coordinating agent for those fighting the liberal takeover of the Episcopal Church." Their membership comprised corporate bodies and included some twenty church societies, monastic communities, and independent publications. When the national Church approved the ordination of women in 1976 (as of January 1, 1977), the Fellowship began its formal withdrawal. In 1977 the Church Congress met in St. Louis and drafted the Affirmation of St. Louis. In 1978 the first four bishops were consecrated at Denver. In 1990 there were over 400 churches or meeting places in all fifty states, five Canadian provinces, Puerto Rico, Mexico, and Haiti.

Membership had already begun to drain away from the Episcopal Church as early as the 1960s. The F.C.C. accelerated the loss, which is now coupled with the daily exodus of disgruntled individuals who join other churches or sit disconsolately in limbo. The threat of the Episcopal Synod of America to withdraw, with its many thousands of churchmen, if a female bishop is forced upon congregations wanting male Episcopal visitors from outside their diocese, becomes more and more dire.

But, we must ask, what is a traditionalist? He (or she) sees himself (or herself) as a member of the Church *as a body*, one who adheres to the long-standing values, customs, and traditions of that corporate group, not one who promotes his (or her) individual tastes or society's dictates. A traditionalist conserves the framework of his church's beliefs while yet exhibiting a willingness to be personally conciliatory where charity demands. A traditionalist is, therefore, a non-fanatical, reasonable conservative. To be conservative, then, is, in the words of economist Michael Oakeshott, in his essay entitled "On Being Conservative," "to prefer the tried to the untried, fact to mystery, the actual to the possible; . . . to acquire and to enlarge will be less important than to keep, to cultivate and to enjoy; the grief of loss will be more acute than the excitement of novelty or promise."[5]

There is tension between liberals and traditionalists. The former accuse their conservative counterpart as overly rigid. The latter insist that liberals never have to explain their actions or apologize. I have tried in the following pages to explain some aspects of both sides.

My mistake has always been to take the Church utterly seriously—at its very word—to believe that it believed what it proclaimed. This was not naive of me; it was, in fact, what the Church had always expected. We can only hope that the Church will recapture that belief in itself so that it may persuade others of its sincerity. These are grim times for the Episcopal Church. But maybe Gilbert Chesterton was right when he said, "It is only when everything is hopeless that hope begins to be a strength."

To the Church I say *ultima forsan*, "it's later than you think."

And I reluctantly add *ultimum vale*, "farewell for the last time."

Donald D. Hook

PROLEGOMENON

Despite a continuing decrease in membership in the Episcopal Church, to all outward appearances there is no grave problem facing the denomination.

The reason for this obvious contradiction is that, for most people, no recognizable problem in the church exists at a level higher than the parish. If the buildings are still standing and occupied, there is no particular concern on the part of the average parishioner even if there may indeed have been a drop in membership or attendance. Sometimes the loss is imperceptible; sometimes it is disregarded; sometimes it is compensated for by combining services, thus obscuring the damage. Of course, losses show up through reduction in pledge income, but most parishioners have little to do with the financial side of their church. Calls for more money go out regularly; but this has always been the case, and people are used to ignoring infringements on their pocketbooks.

Most disturbances of importance in the church are reported in the secular press, not at the parish level. Apparently, not many people read about them, or if they do, they do not comprehend their significance or connect them with their parish. They see them as something outside their experience, particularly if a matter of theology or polity is involved. Most church people of whatever denomination leave such matters to the clergy. There is an element of trust here. Unfortunately, there is now a growing suspicion that it was ill-placed.

For most people "the church" is their parish. There they can satisfy their need for fellowship, obtain Christian education for their children, sing in the choirs, work in special money-making projects, serve on the altar guild — whatever — and it is all right there. Some like to

work with church finances, help on the property committee, participate in layreading, or teach in Church School.
Why should they worry about the national church's involvement in Latin America, the ordination of women,
or even the consecration of the world's first female
bishop in the faraway Diocese of Massachusetts?

What worried parishioners more than anything else
was the introduction of the 1979 revision of the Book of
Common Prayer. The prayer book studies that preceded
the official adoption of the 1979 Prayer Book were
sources of tension and heated argument, and when the
book appeared, there were still many who found it at least
partly objectionable. The Prayer Book was one of those
issues that would not go away, because the people were
constantly exposed to the modernized language through
attendance at services.

Some objections by the people were obviously dealt
with thoughtfully, but others were probably ignored or
filed away. Of course, objections can be ill-founded and
less than thoughtful. The Prayer Book makers themselves no doubt looked upon inexpert, lay criticism as
worth little. During the trial use period many people told
me they could not shake the notion that the format had
already been decided, and it was just a matter of going
through the motions of trying it out on the people. What
the Prayer Book revisers never understood was that the
people did not want a new prayer book — period — never
mind the details.

Be all that as it may, the 1979 Prayer Book was
adopted as the *primary* official instrument of worship.
However, the right to continue to use the 1928 Prayer
Book was authorized by both the House of Bishops and
the House of Deputies at the Denver Convention in
1979. This resolution has been left unchanged by subsequent conventions in 1982, 1985, and 1988. Any parish
rector or priest-in-charge has the right to allow his pa-

rishioners a choice of prayer book. The Gallup poll and other surveys indicate that up to 80% of Episcopalians wish to have a choice between prayer books. But permission has often been denied on the basis that the presence of two prayer books would disrupt unity.

Unity has indeed been disrupted, but for a different reason. An entire national group, the Prayer Book Society, now exists to further the acceptance of the 1928 as an alternative service book. The national church would have been better off in many ways if it had promoted the use of both prayer books, for now the issue is seen and treated by the Prayer Book Society as only one of several major threats to traditionalism in the church.

The issue of the ordination of women reared its head in 1974 when a group sought and achieved illegal ordination in Philadelphia. For many, this was the wrong way to go about the matter, and even some of the hierarchy grumbled a bit. As usual, the newspapers and national magazines brought the matter to the attention of the public. Church people as a whole were scarcely aware of what had happened and overlooked the incident for what it could — and did — become. There was no attempt in adult discussion groups to examine the issue. Few sermons against the idea were preached. One ran the risk of being tagged a bigot if one objected too stringently, for the incident took place within the context of national feminism.

Unknown to the membership at large, seminaries had been accepting large numbers of women. Some were doing so in order to bolster their enrollments, already sagging under a continuing loss of male students. Some were doing so either because they believed that women could achieve legal ordination sooner if they were able to attack the issue in significant numbers, and some — let's be fair — because they honestly believed women have as much right in the priesthood as men. Most of the female students were older persons who were changing careers. They were not entering seminary directly out of undergraduate school, as most men had done. They did not achieve postulant status through their parish, and were, therefore, virtually invisible to the grassroots churches. By the time 1976 rolled around, and the hierarchy legalized female ordination, the people were handed a *fait accompli.*

The parochial clergy fretted over whether this issue might split their parish churches. Individually, they worried lest their bishop might pressure them into taking a woman aboard as deacon, curate, or assistant to the rector. They need not have angonized for one minute about a rupture in their church, but they did have to face up to the fact that there would be fewer and fewer places for men in the profession. Only a handful of clergy uttered a peep about the possibility that the move to ordain women might split the national church.

If the movement for women's ordination was planned, it could not have been better conceived: the utilization of older women — radicals mainly — under no one's control, nobody's children. The former stigmas now worn by seminarians became intimidating badges of acceptance; a vanguard test action was followed by success, and an invisible cadre materialized. Further success was assured because the participants were now recognized as individuals and women, some assuredly lesbians, making rejection impossible.

Female Episcopal seminarians had the support of other denominations. During the decade 1977-1987 the number of women graduating with M.Div. degrees increased 224%. In 1972 women accounted for only 10.2% of seminarians, but by 1987 they constituted 27.4% of all seminary students. Three years later, women now make up approximately 43% of seminarians (341 females versus 453 males), according to the Church Deployment

Office and reports from individual seminaries. The Church Deployment Office further reports that there have been approximately 8000 parochial clergy during the last three years, of whom at present 1446 are ordained females (965 priests, 481 deacons), resulting in 18% female clergy in the United States.[6]

From the beginning, the scene was being set for a female bishop. By dint of having ordained women to the diaconate, the die was inexorably cast for ordination to the next two clerical ranks. And it was true; there was no trouble whatsoever in ordaining women to the priesthood. In fact, the bishops proclaimed that their earlier grumbling had been in error, and they quickly regularized the illegal ordinations.

Achieving the third and last step was a problem of a different order, for to consecrate a female bishop was to tamper with apostolic succession and possibly to isolate the Episcopal Church from its sister provinces in the Anglican Communion as well as from the Roman and Eastern bodies. What was needed was a controversial — and therefore, acceptable — candidate.

Again, the planning was flawless, if, indeed, it was conscious — and we will only know that for a fact if there is a latter-day confession of conspiracy. The rexall: Find a black woman of innate pugnacity with a history of radical action who is as minimally qualified as possible and elect her in the most liberal diocese in the country. It was a foolproof formula; success would be guaranteed. No large numbers of bishops would object, for they would be tarred with the stigmas of bigotry and conservatism.

And, of course, it worked. Except for a small number of courageous bishops, whose actions are examined in the book, and the laity who continue to offer their support to them, the church at large predictably accepted this unprecedented step.

In this connection, it is important to realize that people often have a public and a private stance. Publicly, if watched, they will be friendly and accepting of all changes. Americans, for example, want desperately to be liked. Privately, people will be more selective in their associations and reactions. What they claim to dislike about the church they will confess to close friends, but not to the public at large.

There were other factors at work to assure the success of the venture. American society pits youth against the aging, and since biology makes certain that youth will overcome the elderly, it is not a fair contest. To those who maintain that even youth becomes older and disappears, it is less and less certain today that the middle-aged have shucked their youthful liberal values.

Secondly, the clergy understandably want to keep their jobs. The ministry is no longer jackleg employment, and salary and benefits are not to be sneezed at. Too much grousing will assure an early retirement. There are also clergy who do not wish to face up to the many changes swirling all about them. To do so would be to compromise basic beliefs and commitments from decades back. Furthermore, most Episcopalian clergy are married. Why would they wish to jeopardize their family relationships by opposing female ordination?

Thirdly, despite representation at diocesan and convention levels, the laity have little power except the power to remove themselves. After all, lay representation is a small fraction of the whole. The laity must contend with the entire House of Bishops, plus all the clerical delegates. Of course, if the laity leave in sufficient numbers, somebody will notice; but, as we have noted earlier, there is a built-in reluctance to resign from one's home parish. Moreover, there is the fear of embarrassment, ridicule, and rejection by liberals.

Fourthly, there is the steamroller effect. If, as fast as one change appears on the scene, another is in the making — and another and another — the people will not have the stamina to examine each change and still take care of their day-to-day work and needs. In twenty months, from February 1988 to October 1989, I can recall from my own vantage point alone Harris's consecration, the illegal licensing of Congregational ministers to administer the chalice, the spectacle of the Presiding Bishop concelebrating with a Lutheran bishop, the reception of a UCC member without confirmation, the written invitation to open communion — by a female deacon no less — and assorted statements from several bishops instructing those who do not like the way the church is "to get out." Thousands have, thank you very much.

These bishops say the church needs updating. This is code for "secularizing." One of their spokesmen, Edwin G. Wappler, in his essay, "Anglicans and the New Morality," is at least honest in his celebration of situation ethics, about which he has this to say: "It is the first attempt at a systematic statement of morality which takes as its basis the pragmatic, empirical, relativistic, and personalistic stance of liberalism rather than the rationalistic, deductive, absolutist and principle-centered framework of traditional thought."[7]

That explains a lot. But do read on. There is more that needs explaining.

CHAPTER I

The Problem: Its Nature

"The Episcopal Church has the greatest arsenal of all churches, but has never fired a shot."

— *Billy Sunday*

Paramount among the various missions of any organized religion is the assurance of truth of belief, of doctrinal stability, in the face of secular threats and competition from other, similar religious bodies. For some adherents, change is welcome as long as it can be justified by interpretation based upon scripture, revelation, or action on the part of some member of the Godhead. For others, religious truth is lodged indelibly in pronouncements and interpretations of the distant past, whose applications are valid for all times and under all circumstances. For still others, change is primarily considered salutary if it appears to benefit society at large. The church is then left to rationalize its position vis-a-vis its doctrines.

If these are accurate assumptions, one more must be appended as axiomatic: that the more distant the change, the more acceptable it is. A corollary: The more *frequent* the changes for whatever reasons, the less they are tolerated.

It is precisely the confluence of these notions that has produced chaos in the Episcopal Church in the United States (ECUSA). Where changes in doctrine have occurred in the relative obscurity of the past, they are not only tolerated; they are treated, either consciously or unconsciously, as legitimate pieces of tradition. Where changes have been more proximate to present-day experience, have had disputably beneficial social effects, and have occurred in quick succession, they have been viewed with considerably more suspicion. If a new doctrine strikes many as running counter to earlier doctrines, the hierarchy — or other policymakers — are forced to rationalize the new position and, if possible, to invoke some supernatural component as warrantor.

All these steps preceded or co-occurred with changes in the doctrine and discipline of the ECUSA in the last two decades. What tranquillity existed seems now to be forever shattered — at least for those living amidst the changes. One can only surmise what judgment the perspective of centuries will provide.

The specific changes enacted which have caused so much personal and corporate self-examination are the ordination of women since 1976 as deacons and priests, and now, since February 1989, also as bishops and the revision of the 1928 Prayer Book in 1979. True to thesis, the hullabaloo that immediately ensued died down after a few years, but, except for those — and they were legion — who summarily left the church for some other or became lapsed Episcopalians, the hard-core residue of resisters solidified their position as new threat upon new threat amounted up. The bottom line today shows a church in near schism, suffering a loss of over one million members since 1960, the deposition of priests in disagreement, the renunciation by many priests of their vows, the decimation of male seminarians, and the proliferation of female students. At every stage of the process, the bishops of the church have rationalized the changes by appeal to the *absence* of prohibitive scripture and by assurances that it was not they who promulgated the changes, but the Holy Spirit Himself.

A. The Church as an Artifact of Society

The New Testament Church began, not as an institution, but as a fellowship in Jesus Christ. It had no formal structure such as that which it possesses today, regardless of denomination. Paul's letters to various groups reveal the extent to which an associated life, in which the disciples were linked to one another and to those whom they influenced, created and sustained this new organism. They saw themselves as constituting a virtual "living body of Christ." Few can deny that this spiritual alliance has persisted throughout the centuries.

The Christian Church has found root on every continent on earth, and its presence is felt universally from the local level to the highest halls of government. It is a world community, embracing many languages and races and exceeding all other organizations in influence. Today its institutional status is undoubted. Not only does the Vatican as a state provide convincing proof of the Church's prevalence and potency, but the smaller manifestations of that same power, albeit in a different form, appear at diocesan, even parish level and from denomination to denomination, for the "Church" can be defined in different ways.

One has less difficulty in seeing the "church" as an institution when the body is Roman, Eastern Orthodox, or Anglican than when it is Protestant. Among the former, there is a recognizable and responsible hierarchy whose control is both ecclesiastical and political. Among Protestants, although there are some churches — notably the Swedish Lutheran Church and, from the standpoint of strict polity, the United Methodist Church — that superficially resemble the Catholic groups, there exists no clear agreement on the nature of the "Church." For all "churches," however, theological and sociological terms apply. All can be considered institutions subject to all the regulations and limitations associated with secular organizations.

Like all institutions, the Church has tended to ossify, to become inflexible, rigid, unchanging. Of course, some might prefer other adjectives, such as steadfast, dependable, resolute. In any event, the point is that institutions are not generally thought of as pacesetters, as instruments of change or, as some might say, of progress. For change we need always to look to individuals with vision, courage, even effrontery. Their form varies from prophet to social reformer, and they are often selfless, dedicated Christians whose motives are thoroughly altruistic. Whenever these changes are deemed important enough, they are conserved by the institution. Many see any resistance to change as inhibitive to progress; they would presumably allow *all* changes to be ratified and retained by the church. Typically, the church has filtered out those changes it deemed transient, of little long-term consequence, dangerous to the faith, destructive to its constituents, and detrimental to its relations with other religious bodies.

Times have changed. Under enormous pressure beginning in the 1960s, a time of tremendous and far-reaching social unrest, churches of various stripe suffered a decline in prestige and influence on the national scene. Membership and attendance declined toward the middle of the decade, and the churches sought ways to reinstate their authority. The major clue lay in the success with which the churches had participated in the civil rights movement. It is safe to say that at no time since the years of Prohibition had the churches wielded so much social power. Some might say it went to their heads.

The emphasis on the "social gospel," which dominated U.S. organized Protestant religion in the early part of this century and which appeared to die out, has been restored in the churches of today. Its form is different.

The preachers no longer rail against the evils of drink and tobacco; they do not even particularly inveigh against the scourge of drugs. Instead, they concern themselves with an enlargement of the "social gospel," to include all family matters, racial problems, economic concerns, international relations, and education at every level.

This so-called social gospel did not originate in the United States, nor was it in the beginning a Protestant phenomenon. In the early Church it was an apocalyptic message. The evils of this world would be canceled by the intervention of the supernatural--that is, when Christ came again. There is no evidence that the Church saw its task as remaking the world. It certainly did not encourage the application of human creativity to the construction of a Christian world. In fact, it was quite content to leave the world as it was, complete with all its injustices and inequities, with ignorance, with slavery, with war.

The Church has seldom been in the forefront of effecting social change. Historically, the Church has been slow to act. It has waited until society has clearly indicated its desire to follow a certain course and only then offered its sanction. In fact, it is usually highly resistant to ideas which seem in the beginning to run counter to the perceived doctrines and standards of organized religion. As one example among many, Galileo, who espoused the Copernican view that the sun constitutes the center of the universe, ran afoul of Pope Paul V and was condemned in 1616 by the Congregation of the Index for teaching "a proposition expressly contrary to Holy Scripture." In the nineteenth century there was the equally renowned conflict over Darwin's theory of evolution. Eventually, though, the Church gives its approval to any and all practices considered by the majority to be crucial to their welfare. From the standpoint of society, most of the practices for which church approval is tacitly sought are perceived as largely secular and pragmatic in nature--witness such issues as birth control, abortion, and education, to name only a few. The Church, however, regards all these, and many others, as rightfully within its purview. It contends that Jesus Christ came not only to save souls but to regenerate society.

Over the centuries the former objective has dominated Church action. In the early days Christians were only rudimentarily organized, often persecuted, and spent much time preserving their lives. They were in no position to apply for sweeping social changes. When the organization of the Church became more elaborate, more nearly complete, individual or even group action on the part of the masses remained ineffective. To oppose the Church was risky spiritually and physically. Most of the masses wallowed in ignorance for centuries on end. That ignorance included illiteracy, leading to ignorance of the world and the history of the Church. The clergy were only slightly less ignorant of the natural world, but they wielded their knowledge of the Church like a club over the heads of the people.

By the onset of modern times the Church had become immensely wealthy, rigid, authoritarian, despotic, and exploitative. It owned huge tracts of property, collected exorbitant rents, brooked no doctrinal criticism, exercised its authority through an aristocratic and monarchical hierarchy, coerced conformist belief, and robbed its people under the guise of simony. Little wonder that the next century produced a majority who wrought the most sweeping ecclesiastical changes in the history of Christianity. Great wonder that, viewed from the perspective of almost twenty centuries of mistakes, cruelty, the sanctioning of slavery, the support of the privileged classes — in general, the obstruction of what most would call social progress — the Church has managed to survive the scrutiny of thoughtful people. There are two reasons for its survival: It is, indeed, an artifact of society, a creation of man in its structure; but, many would contend, it is also, in its essentials, a creation of

Christ. The tension between these notions gives the Church its dynamic quality. Were it only of Christ, it could have no adherents. Were it only of man, it could have no future. The perpetual problem remains: What role should man take through the church organization he has constructed to effect social and ecclesiastical change, and how are the people to recognize supernatural intervention when it is allegedly a part of this same organization?

B. The Chicago-Lambeth Quadrilateral

If it has not been obvious all along, a distinction has been made between "the Church" and "churches." The former is to be understood as that New Testament concept of which Christ is the Head. It is composed of believers who are united to Christ in a living, active faith. The "churches" are the separate confessions, or denominations.

If this explanation suffices for the "exterior" aspect of the organization, what about the foundation upon which it rests?

Of course, there will be different answers to go with different churches. Yet, we may ask, is there some agreed-upon minimum, some standard, by which we may judge most denominations? Or, at the very least, are there basic statements that might apply, on the one hand, to the Catholic communions, and, on the other hand, to others that have greater relevance for the Protestant churches?

The Chicago-Lambeth Quadrilateral can broadly apply to both Catholic and Protestant confessions. It identifies the human organization of the Church, and it establishes Christ as the originator.

In 1870 an American Episcopal priest, William Reed Huntington, Rector of Grace Church, New York City, published his book, *The Church Idea: An Essay Towards Unity*, in which he set forth "the absolutely essential features of the Anglican position." This position, he asserted, was identical with that of the historic Catholic Church. He explained it in terms of a "quadrilateral," a fourfold platform which could be the basis for unity by the Anglican Communion. The four points consisted of the Holy Scriptures as the Word of God, the Apostles' and Nicene Creeds as the rule of faith, the two major sacraments of Baptism and Holy Communion, and the historic episcopate as the keystone of governmental unity. The theory was not new; it was inherent in many other pronouncements and assumptions from years before. What was new was the conciseness of the statement, which made it a handy basis for discussion and action.

In 1886, at a meeting of the General Convention in Chicago, the statement was approved by declaration. At the next Lambeth Conference at London in 1887, it was reaffirmed, thus attaining, in 1888, its name, "The Chicago-Lambeth Quadrilateral." In 1892 it was formally adopted by the House of Deputies. Although it established the great similarity among the ancient Catholic groups, its fourth point referring to the episcopate tended to deal out the Protestant churches. Thus, it became both a unifying force and a contentious statement. Many today see the quadrilateral as the major vehicle for preserving Catholic order in the Anglican Communion and furthering relations with Rome and the Orthodox Church. Many more are unaware of its existence. Just as many would not let it stand in the way of some pan-Protestant unity at the expense of true ecumenism.

In 1920, after much discussion and many revisions, the quadrilateral assumed the following form:

We believe that the visible unity of the Church will be found to involve the whole-hearted acceptance of:

The Holy Scriptures as the record of God's revelation of Himself to man, and as being the rule and ultimate standard of faith; and the Creed commonly called Nicene, as the sufficient statement of the Christian faith, and either it or the Apostles' Creed as the Baptismal confession of belief.

The divinely instituted sacraments of Baptism and the Holy Communion, as expressing for all the corporate life of the whole fellowship, in and with Christ.

A ministry acknowledged by every part of the Church as possessing not only the inward call of the Spirit but also the commission of Christ and the authority of the whole body.

Of all the points, the fourth has been the most controversial, for it expresses an exclusivity eliminating those ministries not deriving from St. Peter and the other apostles. The form it originally assumed in 1888 is the one most generally accepted by all segments of the Anglican Communion and reads as follows:

IV. The Historic Episcopate, locally adapted in the methods of its administration to the varying needs of the nations and peoples called of God into the unity of His Church.

Before we can comment on point four as a barrier to union with Protestants or, as the case may be, how its loss or adulteration will affect Anglican relations with Rome and the Orthodox, we need to clarify what the historic episcopate is in importance equal to that of the Bible, creeds, and sacraments. For that we need to return to the earliest time of the Church, to its establishment by Christ Himself. For proof we rely on the other three points of the quadrilateral: the Scriptures as a divinely inspired record of Christ's actions, including His establishment of Baptism and the Last Supper as sacramental acts, and the ratification of those actions in the historic creeds as set down by the Church Fathers.

Chapter II

The Problem: Its Genesis

"Of all the horrid, hideous notes of woe, Sadder than owl-songs or the midnight blast, Is that portentous phrase, 'I told you so.'"

— Byron

Jesus was a Jew and fulfilled all the practices normally expected of Jews. He had no intention of destroying anyone's faith in Judaism; rather, He came, by His own statement, as reported in Matthew 5:17, ..."not to destroy the law, or the prophets ... but to fulfill [it]." He was a regular attender at worship in the synagogue, and His followers continued this practice. In Chapters 13, 14, and 15 of Acts we learn, for example, that Paul and Barnabas attended the synagogues in the cities of the Diaspora. What would be more natural than that synagogue worship and organization should become the model for developing Christian worship and polity? In fact, an examination today of Christian liturgy reveals many similarities with long-held Hebrew practices.

Of immediate interest in a discussion of the development of the Christian clergy is the model set by the officers of the synagogue, a local body of elders, prominent citizens respected for their wisdom and devotion to God. We read in Acts 21:17-18: "And when we were come to Jerusalem, the brethren received us gladly. And the day following Paul went in with us unto James; and all the elders were present." In Acts 14:23 we read: "And when [Paul and Barnabas] had ordained them elders in every church, and had prayed with fasting, they commended them to the Lord, on whom they believed." Surely, such passages teach us that the apostles considered themselves the leaders who possessed the authority to ordain others who would lead individual congregations well outside the confines of Jerusalem. In the *Decree on the Pastoral Office of Bishops in the Church,* Vatican II began its theological statement on bishops with Jesus's promise in John 20:21: "As my Father hath sent me, even so send I you." Does this action not create *presbyteroi*? Were not the apostles acting as bishops when they ordained these men elders? After all, the apostles were eyewitnesses to the resurrection and responded to a mission given by the risen Christ.

On his way to Jerusalem, Paul advises a congregation in Acts 20:28: "Take heed therefore unto yourselves, and to all the flock, over the which the Holy Ghost hath made you overseers, to feed the church of God, which he hath purchased with his own blood." In his letter to Titus, he explains in Chapter 1:5: "For this cause left I thee in Crete, that thou shouldest set in order the things that are wanting, and ordain elders in every city, as I had appointed thee." And, in Titus 1:7, he equates bishops (*episcopoi*) with elders: "For a bishop must be blameless, as the steward of God ..." In his *Epistle to the Trallians* Ignatius (died *c.*117), the self-described Bishop of Syria, maintained: "When you are in subjection to the bishop as to Jesus Christ . . . it is necessary that you should do nothing without the bishop, but be ye also in subjection to the presbytery." And, he added: "Likewise, let all respect the deacons as Jesus Christ, even as the bishop is also a type of the Father, and the presbyters as the council of God, and the college of Apostles." Does this statement not presage the threefold ministry of bishops, priests, and deacons?

It can be asserted that Christ did not really ordain the Twelve Apostles because, in spite of the practice in Palestinian Judaism, the New Testament contains no unambiguous record of His having laid his hands upon them. Based on such lack of evidence, feminists have therefore contended that there is no explicit proof that He excluded women from the ordained ministry. One defect in this argument is that we would limit Christ in His method of commissioning His successors by assuming that He would feel constrained to use the laying on of hands as the one acceptable technique of transmitting His authority. Despite the argument that Christ was [merely] "fulfilling the Jewish [religious and cultural] law" by appointing only men as His disciples and apostles, or that He was adhering to a metaphysical hierarchical relationship between the spiritual and the secular as mirrored in such dichotomies as spirit and matter, human beings and animals, and men and women, there is abundant evidence that Jesus was always one to play the rebel and assert God's truth whenever that truth was in opposition to the understanding of mere people. If He had wished to make the point that women were, for whatever reason, authorized to serve as His apostles, it is logical to assume he would have done so. It is more reasonable to hypothecate that He transmitted His pastoral authority because of divine will. In principle, the ministry established by Christ seems to correspond to the Incarnation and the sacraments in that all three enjoy the security of a divine commission.

A. The 1960s

Women have served in various capacities in the Church over all the centuries of its existence, and the Church has no doubt been the richer for it. From the nun to the altar guild member to the Sunday school teacher to the housewife-volunteer, there is no accounting how much gets done in a church today all because of its female members. It is largely also the women who write the checks—perhaps not the biggest ones, but the ones that sustain the operation. On a day-to-day basis, without women attending services many churches would be almost empty. It is amazing that it took nearly 2000 years for women to realize what power they could wield over their churches. They said at first: "We've done everything else, let us serve on vestries, boards, councils. Let us occupy any position in our church that a man can hold." And it was done. Then they said, "We are doing everything else that a man can do in our church, let us be ordained." And it was done. But much was also undone.

Women's pleas for opportunities of service with authority and power would have fallen on deaf ears — as they had when sporadically voiced in the past — but for the tenor of the times. Cracks had begun developing in church walls decades before the 1960s when a number of mainline Protestant denominations ordained a few women. The number ordained increased, but apparently reached no threatening limits, because no serious objections were raised. The idea spread to the Episcopal Church and even to the Roman Church where, in its earliest and most believable form, nuns began to seek ordination.

Certainly, by 1968 society was unlearning how to say no to anything. Begun by radical college students, a revolutionary movement spread from the campuses to the cities, to Washington and the nation. Fear among the general populace was rampant. The radicals asserted that they would employ force to achieve their objectives — and followed through with their threats. They bombed buildings on campuses and in cities, robbed banks, kidnapped persons, lobbied against all conservative measures in law and government, and eschewed all traditions except those benefiting the downtrodden and forgotten. The impetus had been the much-hated, much-feared war in southeast Asia, and the object of their hatred the so-called "military-industrial complex," but when radical action, including refusal to serve in the armed forces, failed to attain its objectives quickly, the young people of the country turned against society at large and spewed their venom in many directions. Caught in the spray were virtually all time-honored institutions, including all educational assumptions and theological assertions.

Some people ran scared and hid from all the mayhem; many more joined the movement out of fear of retribution if they disagreed. A smaller number resisted the demagoguery and totalitarianism — unfortunately, sometimes with similar methods. Others hitched a ride on the movement's back, seeing a chance of furthering their own objectives or of acting altruistically. The first of the piggy-backers was the civil rights movement, and the second was the women's liberation movement. To make this assertion is not to be cynical; both organizations had valid complaints against society.

The disruptions continued until the mid-seventies, when they rather suddenly ceased on a large scale. All of the radicals had grown older; some had become more introspective. But everyone had had a taste of freedom limited only by one's morals. There was a point, of course, where one could get in trouble with the law, if only temporarily, but legal ingenuity usually sufficed to help one avoid that point. Those who had at first felt uncertain about confronting society with their personal agendas now felt emboldened. More and more such people saw themselves as anything but radicalized; they considered themselves entitled. The largest and most important group in this struggle was the women of America.

B. COCU

Some have had the playful audacity to pronounce the above acronym "cuckoo," in a not-so-playful attempt to downgrade the seriousness of its objectives and to predict the certainty of its failure. To these people many others would say: Take them seriously; they are a dangerous lot.

Although the history of the non-Anglican, non-Roman, non-Orthodox churches in the United States is primarily that of divisions into more and more distinct units — some handbooks list as many as 250 separate denominations — and although there have been, over the years, a number of re-formations and alliances, there has never been such a long-lasting determination to re-unite — in most senses, the wrong word since the partner churches were never one except in the most basic respects — as under the aegis of the Consultation on Church Union. That COCU wants to see its mission as God-commissioned is obvious from the high-sounding, idealistic language of the periodic reports. Furthermore, one senses a maudlin attempt to justify every proposal by pointing out how humble the authors are.

The movement was born on Nob Hill, in San Francisco, on a foggy, breezy December 4, 1960. In a lengthy sermon, "A Proposal Toward the Reunion of Christ's Church," preached in Grace Cathedral, the Rev. Dr. Eugene Carson Blake, Stated Clerk of the United Presbyterian Church in the U.S.A., urged careful study of the possibilities of the union of certain selected reformed bodies and the Episcopal Church. Responding to this challenge, the 173rd General Assembly of the United Presbyterian Church in the U.S.A. invited the Episcopal Church to join them in issuing invitations to the Methodist Church and the United Church of Christ for a meeting in 1961.

Initially, in all, there were six denominations involved: the United Presbyterian Church in the U.S.A., the Methodist Church, the United Church of Christ, the Evangelical United Brethren, the Christian Churches (the Disciples of Christ), and the Episcopal Church. Only the Polish National Catholic Church, with whom the Episcopal Church was in full communion, declined to participate fully. Each denomination, regardless of size or influence, sent nine representatives to each meeting. The plan was to convene annually in a plenary session; interim reports for later presentation were prepared by appointed committees throughout the year. The stumbling blocks were enumerated at the start, and, it must be said, most took off their rose-colored glasses while reading them. The impediments included agreement on the nature of the ordained ministry and the essence of the Eucharist and other sacraments. Everything was to be studied and implemented with a view to establishing a super-church that was "truly catholic, truly evangelical, and truly reformed."

Some people were, and still are, puzzled by the underlying, unspoken definitions of these crucial words, although the order indicates a dichotomy — catholic/evangelical — of which both constituents are in need of reform. In charity, we assume that, generally speaking, the incipient new church, in its wisdom, wishes to incorporate the "best" features — as currently defined — of the non-Roman, non-Orthodox denominational threads of U.S. Christianity. Throughout the reports a conscious avoidance of such possibly offending terms as bishop, priest, Mass, saint, and the naming of sacraments other than Baptism and the Lord's Supper (or Holy Communion or Eucharist) is all too evident. The reconstruction of this Humpty-Dumpty is going to be very difficult.

Which raises the question for us: Why should selected denominations try to unite? (Oddly, this question was not voiced by COCU.) Admittedly, the Bible speaks of "one faith" (Rom. 1:5, Eph. 4:11-13, 2 Tim. 4:7, Tit. 1:1, Rev. 14:12, 1 John 5:4, Eph. 6:16), and tradition and the creeds speak of the "Catholic faith," but the atomism of post-Reformation times came much later. If each of the selected denominations is to consider each of the others on a par with itself as a holder of equally valid faith — as proclaimed in many COCU reports — why unite? Is it for pragmatic reasons — for example, to wield more power both from the top and sideways against perceived inimical forces; to achieve a leveling of class differences; to further individual notions of God's message; or even to purchase supplies in bulk at a healthy discount?

Why, indeed, should a group of reasonably like-minded churches — the Presbyterians, Methodists, Evangelical United Brethren, Disciples, Congregationalists — imagine themselves united with the Episcopal Church? Why would the Episcopal Church, at that time the one unfragmented body out of the whole group, want to unite with such a disparate collection? Why did the Presbyterians, a church disunited in itself — there were the Presbyterian Church in the U.S.A., the Presbyterian Church in the U.S., the Presbyterian Church, U.S., and the United Presbyterian Church — hope to accomplish something outside their denomination that they could not bring off at home?

In December 1988, at its 17th Plenary session, COCU devised a plan for the formation of a "covenant communion of the churches" in the form of a resolution. This resolution was unanimously passed by the membership and sent to all the member churches. Even though this so-called "COCU Consensus" was turned down by the Episcopal Church as lacking "sufficient theological basis for the covenanting acts," the matter will be brought up again in 1991. This document constitutes the basis for merger. It reads:

> RESOLVED: the 17th plenary meeting of the Consultation on Church Union, assembled in New Orleans on December 5-9, 1988, approves the document, CHURCHES IN COVENANT COMMUNION: THE CHURCH OF CHRIST UNITING, and commends it to the participating churches with the request that each church, by formal action, 1) approve this text as the definitive agreement for joining with other participating churches in covenant communion, including the acts sufficient to enable

it, 2) declare its willingness to enter into a relationship of covenant communion with the member churches of the Consultation on Church Union and other churches which similarly approve this agreement and THE COCU CONSENSUS, which is its theological basis, sealed by the proposed inaugural liturgies, and 3) begin to identify for itself such steps and procedures as may be necessary to prepare for the reconciliation of ordained ministries and for entering into covenant communion as set forth in this document.

What prompted the Episcopal Church to join such a group in the first place? What enables such a group to continue after 27 years of running in place?

These are not easy questions to answer. One of the scarier replies to the first question is that the Episcopal Church did not, and does not, recognize the arsenal it maintains. In other words, it was not aware of its bargaining position. Even more frightening is the proposition that the deal-makers, out of sheer ignorance, were willing to sell their, and our, birthright. That there could be such a procession of timid bunglers over all these years boggles the mind — unless, of course — as they would fervently state — they are not bunglers at all but ready responders to messages from the Holy Ghost.

Have there been so few objections to the tenacity of COCU that it has been able to prolong its existence despite its failure from year to year? Yes. And the reason is that the people at large are unaware after so long a time that COCU is still viable. They never quite understood what it was all about in the beginning. When they gained an idea, they were afraid to resist it for fear of being called intolerant, elitist, or conservative. That feeling continues. Furthermore, like commercial messages on TV that are endlessly repeated, the pronouncements from

COCU are no longer heard; they merely influence hearers subliminally.

There are many sub-agendas in COCU, but by the members' own admission, the most worrisome problems have always been the nature of the ordained ministry and its relation to the administration of the sacraments. The matter of whether to ordain women was meticulously sidestepped until the first published collection of reports in 1965 when COCU "urge[d] careful study and clarification of this matter." In the meantime, waiting paid off, for the question has become academic after the Episcopal Church's positive decision in 1976. It is no longer necessary to untangle more basic aspects of the apostolic ministry; the functioning of women priests has essentially negated or overridden those problems.

If any of this is objectionable to the laity, why have they not withheld their monetary support for COCU? Again, they have little knowledge on a regular basis of what is going on behind their backs. Secondly, there is so much else that demands one's attention in a complex modern world, that one despairs of keeping up with what should be a matter of the preservation of the faith — the job of the clergy largely. Why can the clergy not be trusted to guard the faith? (Defining "the faith" is, of course, for many people a debatable matter.) One answer: They first have to guard their jobs.

C. Prayer Book Revision

Coming on the heels of the social upheavals and permissiveness of the 1960s and accompanied by the occasional nuisance of news about COCU, a revision of the beloved 1928 Prayer Book was for many Episcopalians, if not the last, then the penultimate straw on the proverbial camel's back.

Actually, it was as early as the 1950s that much thought was already being given to a major overhaul of the 1928 Prayer Book, but it took the 1960s to provide a favorable atmosphere for such far-reaching changes. In view of the lead taken by the Roman Church during Vatican II (1962-1965) and by continental Protestant scholars, the Anglican Congress in 1963 refined and confirmed guidelines laid down by the Lambeth Conference of 1958. This process began a round of trial services which varied from province to province in time of introduction and in content, culminating in the United States in a new Prayer Book approved in 1979.

Reactions to the new Prayer Book were all over the field, as the responses to the several stages of trial use had been. Some changes had indeed been made in deference to observations and use of trial forms, but now everything was cast in concrete, and many people were unhappy. That just as many were happy with the new book was less true than that just as many were confused.

It is impossible to please everyone with a new Prayer Book. The very first Prayer Book (1549) was seen by many as too conservative, but by just as many others as too radical. However, it is not so important to please a majority as it is to please *a majority of major segments of the church*: active church members and parochial clergy. Scholars may write what they wish; bishops may pontificate. But the people who are close to the *use* of the book must approve.

In a world that had been changing with ever-increasing momentum since the end of World War II, the 1928 Prayer Book represented for millions of Episcopalians a locus of personal, private stability, a dependable flotation device in a swirling sea littered with the flotsam of good and bad ideas. One of the things the people disliked most about the new book was the inclusion of standard, everyday forms of address in Rite II, the Psalms, and allied prayers. Never mind that there was Rite I and its collects and special prayers in traditional language; the very presence of a mechanism to move the people farther from God and back into the sounds of their workaday existence was unpalatable. The people were particularly vehement when expressing their distaste for the non-traditional form of the Lord's Prayer. There is a dichotomy of the sacred and the profane. The two worlds are separate; we mortals can approach an understanding of the sacred only through our human language. Our mistake is to insist on absolute parallelism with our world. To put it another way, liturgical language ought not to have *primarily* a worldly focus, for the divine reality is beyond human experience.

If objections to language are the only substantial ones, as some defenders of the 1979 Prayer Book argue, then there is no real problem. All the church has to do is wait a while, and the furor will die down. In fact, in a couple of decades no one will even remember how the 1928 differed. That is probably true, although the continued resistance on the part of The Prayer Book Society, which now has many more axes to grind than the Prayer Book alone, gives one pause. More pertinent to the general issue of Prayer Book revision are the questions whether a change in language does not often change meaning and whether, in fact, there are not more substantial changes than meet the eye or the ear through language alone. Not only changes in sections, rubrics, and prayers, but the addition or the omission of items can alter meaning, intent, and overall tone of a prayer book.

To put it in modern terms, the first Book of Common Prayer had as its major objective communication. Archbishop Thomas Cranmer advises, in the preface, that the liturgy should be "in suche a language and ordre, as is moste easy and plain for the understandyng, bothe of the readers and hearers." Like that Prayer Book of 430 years before, the 1979 Prayer Book uses that rationale, among others, for replacing the 1928. In the Introduction to his *Commentary on the American Prayer Book*, Marion J.

Hatchett asserts that "the language has been made contemporary and accords with standard modern [American] English usage."[8] The major difference in the two lines of reasoning is that the 1549 book was the first translation of a complete service book into English and the 1979 book was ostensibly an attempt to make the English more understandable, more up-to-date. In the first instance, it was a question of rendering the liturgy out of Latin into another language; in the second instance, it was a matter of making the English "clearer." To be sure, some sort of case can be made for any liturgical language, whether or not it be the language of the people — after all, Old Church Slavic is still used in some Eastern Rite churches, Sanskrit continues as the ritual language of the Northern Buddhist Church, and, until only comparatively recently, Latin was the language of all Roman Catholic churches. Yet, today we tend to think of understanding as implying much more than merely comprehending in some mystical or romantic sense. By "understanding," many today mean not only the denotation of the words but their application to current experience. For others, though, even that is not enough. The mystical-aesthetic aspect should be there, too, and with it, a connection with the past. It need not, it cannot, be the far distant past, such that, like Old or Middle English, genuine comprehension is lost because of utter change of meaning of some words or forms. However, it can be a past which is close enough to preserve most meanings clearly but distant enough to awaken an appreciation for the continuity of the Church in her public celebrations.

It was surely an unspoken awareness of this human need that prompted the revisers of the 1928 Prayer Book to retain most forms of that book in the 1979 Prayer Book, although many features have undergone condensation, revision, and rearrangement. Rite I is not all that jarring to some former devoted users of 1928.

Rite II is quite another matter. Despite all the good that has or may come from language developed by the International Council on English Texts, and despite all the sincere efforts by the many scholars who worked on the 1979 Prayer Book, "the contemporary" language employed is all too often more an odd mixture of old and new, and decidedly not contemporary. Perhaps one should be happy that it is not truly up-to-date, with the many neologisms, speech interrupters, and substandard grammar that characterize casual U.S. talk today; but the language does not strike one as even present-day in a colloquial sense. It looks and sounds more like traditional language that has had the thou's, thee's, thy's, and thine's strained out, into which residue a current word or expression or odd metaphor has been injected. Occasionally, one is overcome by a strange feeling of disrhythm, puzzlement, or amusement.

In his booklet, "The Form of Sound Words," Jerome F. Politzer, President of The Prayer Book Society, wages scholarly attack on a number of aspects of the 1979 Prayer Book. Among the "infelicities" he lists are examples from the psalter, such as: "Save me, O God, for the waters have risen up to my neck."(Psalm 69:1); "A deadly thing, they say, has fastened on him; he has taken to his bed and will never get up again."(Psalm 41:8); "...every night I drench my bed, and flood my couch with tears."(Psalm 6:6); "He struck his enemies on the backside and put them to perpetual shame."(Psalm 78:66). In the 1928 Book of Common Prayer these passages are rendered as follows, in order: "Save me, O God; for the waters are come in, even unto my soul"; "An evil disease, say they, cleaveth fast unto him; and now that he lieth, he shall rise up no more"; "...every night wash I my bed, and water my couch with my tears"; and (Psalm 78:67[*sic*]) "He drave his enemies backward, and put them to a perpetual shame."

There is no doubt that these examples are indeed "infelicities." Unlike Politzer, though, I would make the point that the 1928 is no better. If the intention of the revisers was to clarify or to "felicitate" these passages, they failed. How often the revisers missed their objective I leave to the reader with the fine-toothed comb. This statement does not imply that the 1979 is an utter failure in all respects; neither does it say that the 1928 is a perfect book. It does imply that the 1928 is a less flawed book in respect of majesty of language.

It is not the intention of the present writer to offer a scholarly analysis of the 1979 Book. The average churchman may not read such analyses, anyhow; he operates on the level of feeling. He says to himself: This sounds all right; this does not. Or: This is not what it used to say.

If we look only at the two "major" sacraments, Baptism and Holy Eucharist, since they were part of the bedrock of the Chicago Quadrilateral, we do indeed find that some things don't sound right or aren't the same as they used to be.

The Church has always taught that the doctrine of regeneration is of the essence of the sacrament of Baptism. From the first Prayer Book through the 1928, this essential doctrine of God-given grace was made clear. In the 1928, the word "regeneration" is used no fewer than four times (pp.273-281). In the 1979, the word is totally missing. Except for the use of the words "rebirth" and "reborn" on two occasions, there is no hint of the doctrine. Instead, the rite concentrates on initiation and implies something more like membership in the church. Most users of the 1979 Prayer Book — laity and clergy alike — are not in a position to argue the theological point convincingly. They simply recognize that there has been a change, and they would like someone to tell them why regeneration is no longer of the essence. Was the previous theology in error? Even Marion Hatchett skirts the matter in his *Commentary* and mentions regeneration only once. He reports: "The last half of the nineteenth century was racked by controversy over baptismal regeneration, with both sides often straining the meanings of Prayer Book texts."[9] Hatchett offers many interesting and helpful historical details, including the return of emphasis to public rather than private Baptism, but does not attempt to justify or explain what appears to be a change in doctrine.

The doctrine of regeneration is important to an understanding of the Holy Eucharist, for it is the door in the sacrament of Baptism through which we enter into the fellowship of the reconciled. By means of Baptism we achieve a new relationship with God in Christ. Our sin is washed away, and we are saved from eternal death. This is the beginning of the atonement.

The most prevalent conception of the Atonement is that advanced by St. Anselm (1033-1109), theologian and Archbishop of Canterbury, who, in his *Cur Deus Homo?*, described vicarious atonement this way. God, desirous of the reconciliation of humankind, will pardon people if they will make satisfaction for their sins. But mere people are unable to make satisfaction for their sins, so offensive are their transgressions to the exaltedness of God. Therefore, God, in His infinite mercy, sent His Son to earth to effect the reconciliation. Because He is of the Trinity, God Himself, Jesus Christ took on the sins of humankind and satisfied the Father. By His assumed humanity, His sufferings on earth for all people, and most especially by His Crucifixion, He has redeemed us all if we will but accept Him.

At the center of the Holy Eucharist stands the doctrine of the Atonement, and its backdrop is the Incarnation. With the emphasis now on initiation in the Baptismal rite, it is easy to understand how open communion has become more and more commonplace. Not only do some officiating clergy invite all baptized persons to receive; some even publish the invitation in the bulletin. What is not easy to understand is why the Atonement and the Incarnation are not stressed as natural allies of Baptism. Some churchmen maintain the dilution is a result of the multiplicity of rites, where others see the variety as a very good thing regardless of what is being diluted. There are eight rites now available — seven for use under formal circumstances, one a kind of database called "Order for Celebrating the Holy Eucharist"(p.400) waiting to be filled in by a do-it-yourselfer. This is the rite objectors pin their attention on, for they see it as an allurement to secular and gnostic encroachments.

Here and there throughout the 1979 there is evidence that, for whatever reasons, the Atonement and the Incarnation have been de-emphasized. "Propitiation" has become "perfect offering." In the Prayer of Humble Access (p.337) the end has been omitted: "...that our sinful bodies may be made clean by his body, and our souls washed through his most precious blood..." It is certainly hard to understand why those particular twenty words were eliminated unless it was for a theological reason.

In the Prayer of Thanksgiving (p.339) it is once again puzzling why the revisers would go to the trouble to remove nine words so obviously dealing with the Atonement unless they had a theological objection: "...by the merits of his precious death and passion." Similarly, in all except Rite I the doctrine of the Atonement is marked by its absence. The doctrine of the Incarnation fares no better. In another booklet, "A Form of Godliness," Jerome F. Politzer observes: "[T]he doctrine of the Incarnation as expressed in the teachings of the Real Presence and Eucharistic Sacrifice is made equivocal and ambiguous in Rite II and Form 1 and Form 2. Qualifying phrases are used to give a subjective tone to the terms 'body' and 'blood' of Christ in these rites. There is no way that Form

1 and Form 2 can be considered to be a liturgical sacrifice because there is no prayer of offering of the elements included in them. The Oblation or offering of the consecrated elements is a vital part of the whole consecration prayer. It brings together the thanksgivings and memorials that have gone before and offers them to God by means of the elements of bread and wine, which our Lord chose to represent His sacrifice." There is a danger that the Eucharist has taken on humanistic coloration.

But most worshippers are not immediately concerned with the theological questions attendant upon revision. Their dissatisfactions are of a different order. Those who used to depend upon a single Prayer of Consecration are disturbed by the choice now available, and those who appreciate variety often complain that, in fact, hardly ever is any but Eucharistic Prayer A used. This is a problem met usually by alternating Rite I with Rite II and occasionally substituting one of the other Eucharistic prayers for A. One might contend that it is a problem that could have been solved by a new Prayer Book with only Rite II, supported by the authorization also of the 1928. But, as we have seen, there is inherent objection to the authorization of two prayer books at the same time.

Other objections to the new Prayer Book are too numerous — too trivial? — to list. They fall into the broad category of the unfamiliar and informal. Tortured horse that it is, it is still being beaten: The use of "you" instead of "thou" and "thee" and associated possessive adjectives rankles. "It just doesn't sound like you are talking to God," observed a middle-aged parishioner.

Then there is the Gloria. "I guess it means the same thing," said a young person this time, "but the rhythm is wrong. I feel awkward saying or singing it. And the same goes for the Creed." Then she added, "Maybe it's the punctuation. There's not the same flow." Could one not add to this observation that there is the same uncertainty about the Sursum Corda when we say, "We lift them to the Lord." The celebrant has just used a slightly different verb, "to lift up," not just "to lift." The reply ought to be with the same verb, and "unto" "flows" much better than the stark "to."

What about the Peace? It is as if a button had been pressed. With much turning and twisting, clawing and clutching, people greet one another — whether they want to or not. Admittedly, we are in the midst of corporate worship — actually just before the announcements — but must it be at the expense of the individual? Must one appear that one has just emerged from a trance and has only now seen the persons roundabout? One does not have to answer one's telephone or front door. Why must one have to interrupt one's private devotions? Those who complain about the Peace along these lines are frequently put in their place by those who chalk their attitude up to the basic unfriendliness of Episcopalians. Odd thing is — the Roman Catholics react the same way.

Then there is the proclamation of the mystery of faith smack dab in the middle of the Prayer of Consecration. Shaken out of their devotion, reverie, or slumber, the congregation must bellow forth with the celebrant: "Christ has died. Christ is risen. Christ will come again." True message, fine message that it is, it should not be ejaculatory. It jars.

There follows the Lord's Prayer. It is enormously instructive that here the people absolutely drew the line. There was simply no way they were going to substitute so-called modern English for a prayer that had strengthened them all their lives. In the last ten years, the present writer has attended services in Episcopal and Anglican churches in states spanning the country and in five foreign countries and is yet to hear the modern version. Does insistence upon the old version represent a microcosm of discontent?

For some, of course, Prayer Book revision has not gone far enough. Among that group are feminists and their supporters who, for example, cavalierly change "men"—so much for modern American English!—to "men and women" or "people" or, when beginning the sermon or giving the blessing, unhesitatingly invoke "God, the Father, God, the Mother, God, the Child" instead of using the required formula. In her *Models of God: Theology for an Ecological, Nuclear Age*, theologian Sallie McFague of Vanderbilt Divinity School recommends "Mother, Lover, and Friend." The day following her consecration in February 1989, Bishop Barbara Harris allegedly used the "non-sexist" words "Creator, Redeemer, and Sustainer" (for "Father, Son, and Holy Ghost," in case the meaning is not obvious).

This does not end the litany of complaints nor does it nullify any complaints people had about the 1928. It may mean something is actually wrong or, as we theorized earlier, not enough time has elapsed for everything to become familiar, for people to forget the way it was.

D. Inclusive Language

"Inclusive language" is a mock professional linguistics term that became popular in the 1980s. It comprises aspects of current colloquial usage as well as specialized application in, say, the law and religion. At bottom, inclusive language is, in the broadest sense of the word, a political movement to provide greater linguistic equality for women by attempting to engineer changes in the English language. One could profitably examine a multitude of examples of this trend in modern U.S. English, but our concern is limited to its application to religious language. Unfortunately, there has been a marked lack of rigor in the development of inclusive language for liturgical purposes. It seems not to have occurred to many to solicit the analysis and advice of linguists in the preparation of certain materials, a step no less logical than seeking the aid of chemists in the concoction of a new compound. For general purposes, let us consider a linguistic analysis of the word "God" and its implications for inclusive language.

Feminists' efforts in recent years to eliminate perceived sexist language in American English have met with a surprising degree of success, at least initially. However, it will take many years to witness a codification of any deletions and alterations. Some of the proposed changes have little chance for adoption and may serve only to raise the ire, instead of the consciousness, of the general public.

There are two areas in particular where fundamental changes are not likely in the foreseeable future. One is that of pronouns and related possessive adjectives. The other is the language of the Christian religion as contained in the Bible, prayers, and liturgy.

In October 1983 a committee of the National Council of Churches put together a desexed experimental lectionary in which, among other things, "the Lord God" is rendered as "God the Sovereign One." The implication seems to be, first of all, that "Lord" has masculine overtones, but "God" and/or "the Sovereign One" are neuter (or neutral). In the same lectionary "Father" becomes "God my Mother and Father." Compare the new version with the Revised Standard version:

Revised Standard Version

In the day that the **Lord**

God *made the earth and the*

heavens, when no plant of the

field was yet in the earth and

no herb of the field had yet

sprung up — for the **Lord God**

had not caused it to rain upon

the earth, and there was no

man *to till the ground; but*

a mist went up the earth and

watered the whole face of

the ground--then **the Lord**

God *formed* **man** *of dust*

from the ground, and breathed

into his nostrils the

breath of life; and **man**

became a living being.

Genesis 2:4-7

New Translation

In the day that **God the Sovereign**
One *made the earth and the heavens,*
when no plant of the field was yet
in the earth and no herb of the
field had yet sprung up — for the
Sovereign One *had not caused it*
to rain upon the earth, and there
was **no one** *to till the ground;*
but a mist went up from the earth
and watered the whole face of the
ground — then God the **Sovereign**
One *formed a human creature*
of dust from the ground, and
breathed into the **creature's**
nostrils the breath of life;
and **the human creature** *be-*
came a living being.

Revised Standard Version

At that time Jesus declared,
"I thank **thee, Father, Lord**
of heaven and earth, that
thou hast *hidden these*
things from the wise and under-
standing and revealed them to
babes; yea, **Father,** *for such*
was **thy** *gracious will. All*
things have been delivered
to me by my Father; and no
one knows the **Son** *except*
the **Father,** *and no one*
knows the **Father** *except*
the **Son** *and any one to*
whom the **Son** *chooses to*
reveal **him.**

Matthew 11:25-27

New Translation

At that time Jesus declared,
"I thank **you,** *[***God my Mother***
and] *Father, Sovereign of*
heaven and earth, that **you**
have *hidden these things from*
the wise and understanding and
revealed them to babes; yea,
God, *for such was* **your**
gracious will. All things have
*been delivered to me by [***God***]*
*my Father [***and Mother***]; and*
no one knows the **Child** *except*
God, *and no one knows* **God**
except the **Child** *and any one*
to whom the **Child** *chooses*
to reveal **God.**

Prominent feminists have maintained there is clearly a masculine bias in such appellations for God as "judge, king, lord, master, shepherd, fire, rock, two-edged sword, and father." In an article in *The Way*, entitled "Women's Images of God and Prayer," Jill Robson goes on to say: "These may only be images, metaphors or analogies that we use to speak of God, who is beyond all the images that we can have. But images are powerful. They shape the way we understand and experience the world around us. Moreover, they shape how we understand (and experience) the God whom we do not see."[10] Other, impartial observers note that feminine images of God are, nevertheless, secondary to the more paternal images. Gail Ramshaw-Schmidt, in her article "An Inclusive Language Lectionary" in *Worship*, has given a balanced evaluation of this lectionary in which she lauds the committee for forcing us to think profoundly about the *meaning* of our traditional terminology of God as derived from Jewish culture, but in which she also calls the committee to task for sometimes interpreting obvious metaphors in "a naively literalistic manner." She sees "God the Father and Mother" as an example of that literalistic tendency, but urges us to accept the Sovereign One.[11] Here I would part company with her.

Given the liturgical prevalence of the words "Lord," "God," and "Father," and the likelihood of objections to tampering with such basic, familiar terms, perhaps a short linguistic treatment of these words will prove enlightening. Let it be known from the outset that I make no theological judgments based on personal religious preferences. Secondly, some definitions are in order.

"God" is construed as the monotheistic God of Judaism, Christianity, and Islam, not as one of any pantheon. Specifically, what is meant is the Christian God, the creator and ruler of the universe, the supreme being and guiding entelechy. "God" is also the Christ and one of the Trinity.

"Lord" also means Christ and is equivalent to "God" above.

"Sovereign One" is not hallowed by usage in the Christian faith and must be defined in more general terms: one supreme in power, rank, authority, and independent of all others. It would follow then that whatever the term "Sovereign One" means, it can add nothing in conjunction with God, for God is all that "Sovereign One" is and more. Neither can "Sovereign One" substitute for "Lord" since "Lord" and "God" are one and the same. Furthermore, if "Lord" be objected to as masculine not only in form but also in content because, in the history of mankind most "lords," in the common sense of the word, have been men, the same can be said of "sovereign." If a substitute for "Lord" were seriously deemed necessary, only "God" could qualify. It is an equivalent term and, as referent, neutral (or neuter). Ramshaw-Schmidt disagrees and maintains that the committee's frequent substitution of "God" for the tetragrammaton is "plain and simple mistranslation, and a serious instance, at that." The sense, or reference, of the word will, of course, vary somewhat from individual to individual — and herein undoubtedly lies the problem for feminists. Words have meaning spheres, connotations as well as denotations, and sometimes the connotations take on metaphorical proportions.

A further word of caution is in order here. Metaphors and analogies are not the same — at least not on the surface. In his book, *The Battle for the Trinity*, Donald G. Bloesch states his agreement with St. Thomas Aquinas and Karl Barth "that analogical knowledge is real knowledge, whereas metaphorical knowledge is only intuitive awareness or tacit knowledge. An analogy conveys conceptual content; a metaphor alludes to that which escapes conceptualization. To say that God is a Rock or Fortress is metaphorical, but to call God Father or Lord is analogical. A metaphor connotes a suggested likeness between two things that are manifestly dissimilar, whereas an analogy presupposes an underlying similarity or congruity in the midst of real difference."[12]

If we look more deeply into the matter, we may disagree to some extent with Bloesch. Metaphors are based on ambiguities; that is, they represent an opposition between a literal meaning based on the normal semantic properties of the word in question versus a meaning based on the semantic properties inferred. Analogy is a process by which a word or a form becomes modelled after some existing pattern. The well-known American Bible Society linguist Eugene A. Nida has advised me, in a private communication, that "metaphor does not necessarily elude that which escapes conceptualization, and in terms of semantics, certainly calling God a 'fortress' is essentially no different from calling God 'father.' The only difference is that there are more semantic ties in the second instance. In other words, the analogies are more fully developed, and one might say that semantically there is a greater degree of isomorphism." To put it still another way, given the words "rock" and "fortress," we do not as readily conceptualize God as when we hear or see the word "father." The attributes associated with the inanimate "rock" or "fortress," for all their connotations of solidity, firmness, defense, and protectiveness, are not equal to the qualities of authority and provision of needs as expressed in the animate "father." Nida insists that, among other things, "the presumed provision for offspring ... is a very important element in the concept of God as father—at least insofar as it is developed in the Scriptures."

Still another caution comes to mind. This discussion deals with words that feminists in their search for appropriate *in*clusive language ought to designate as *ex*clusive language. For Judaeo-Christianity is fraught with exclusiveness: a Chosen People, God in history, Redemption for the faithful only, the Trinity of God the Father, God the Son, and God the Holy Spirit. The genesis of the feminist movement in America, and its major successes here in various quarters, may just be misleading some who carry forward to their religion and its language assumptions based on our egalitarian society. Far too many Americans — churchpeople and clergy among them — have become, as Herbert Schlossberg in his *Idols for Destruction* has put it, "so accustomed to deferring to society's norms as *their* norms that anything else seems odd."[13] Furthermore, he says, "humanists who have no special affinity for the message of the church nevertheless welcome whatever help they can get from religious organizations in furthering *their* ends."[14]

The linguistic device of distinctive features is sometimes used in semantic study in order to provide a universal framework for handling meaning. On page 40 is a chart in which the Christian God is described by means of [some] distinctive features. God is viewed as constituting a linguistic ideal, but as "existing" as a process and a conception within an individual or human group context:

Thus, understood in human terms, the "ideal" (A) God is neither male nor female nor human, is abstract, non-material, may or may not be animate, and has no generational, familial, procreative capability. B God differs from A only in possessing maleness and therefore also generational capability. The hoped-for, sought-after C God of altered terminology is both female and male, but in the bargain loses generational capability. If it should be argued that hermaphrodites can produce progeny, or even that the B God could have male and female features reversed to delineate a God as Mother giving "virgin birth" to creation, objections from theology would inundate the logico-linguistic assertions that the verbs to "father" and to "mother" are quite different and that all arguments dealing with the proverbial chicken and egg are doomed to confusion, if not failure.

In his article "Gender and Creed: Confessing a Common Faith" S. Mark Heim brings the question down to this: "[D]oes 'mother' have the same terminological meaning of generation as 'father'? To argue that it cannot have this meaning because women's role in reproduction implies a previous male role is to fall into the very line of thought that the creed itself ruled out in its connotations of the word 'father' — i.e., the dominance of human analogy. (And even human analogy would fail to yield a clear distinction, since 'father' implies a female role just as much as 'mother' implies a male one.) Thus the only possible arguments for exclusively using father language seem to be: (1) Something about the relation of generation is more aptly expressed by 'father' than 'mother'; and (2) there simply are 'revealed metaphors" — mandated ways to speak of the unspeakable — that we must preserve."[15]

The feminists' contention that certain appellations for God are male-slanted and therefore wrong or unfair or inadequate points up clearly that no expression can adequately represent the divine. There are various names for God in the Old Testament. Of all these, the best known is the tetragrammaton YHWH, or Jahweh. The ancient Hebrews considered this name ineffable and in speaking and reading aloud substituted Adonai [my Lord]. The New Testament God has come down to earth in the form of Jesus Christ and established a personal relationship with human beings by dint of a specific theology of Incarnation (with all that involves). A non-linguistic defense of such terms as "Father," "Father, Son, and Holy Ghost," "Son of Man," can thus be mounted. Such terms for the Blessed Virgin Mary as "Queen of Heaven" and "Mother of God," also established in theology and tradition, can be defended as complementing the male side of the deities and creating

```
            Linguistic nature of LORD/GOD (ascended)
   — — — — >        — — — — >        — — — — >
   d e v e l o p i n g   s e m a n t i c   p r o p e r t i e s


        A                  B                  C

    (Ideal)          (As viewed at present   (As sought
                     [and in past?] by       by feminists)
                     feminists and many
                     non-feminists alike)
   - male            + male                 + male
   - female          - female               + female
   - human           - human                - human
   + abstract        + abstract             + abstract
   + non-material    + non-material         + non-material
   + animate         + animate              + animate
   - generational    + generational         - generational
     capability        capability             capability
```

a divine family. But such a set-up militates against addressing God as female or as some androgynous being, for God = Christ ≠ BVM.

For feminists, the issue turns about the word "father" and other words that, in human or traditional terms, seem to imply male exclusiveness or superiority or generality. According to Heim: "[I]t would be consistent with the [Nicene] creed's faith to avoid any gender-linked word for God. According to [another] view, the word 'father' — while not implying that the first person of the Trinity is male (an implication that the Cappadocian fathers, for instance, vehemently deny) — conveys an aspect of trinitarian faith that no other language can express. [Furthermore,] it can be argued historically that the creed's 'father' language is not saying anything about God as known through creation (e.g., extrapolating knowledge of God from knowledge of human fathers), but rather is speaking of God within the Trinity: a subject unknowable and inexpressible save through revealed language. And even in such language, since we know so tenuously that of which we speak, we have a hard time meaning it correctly. To understand 'father' in [purely] human terms is to misunderstand it."[16] To append "mother" is to confound the Church's understanding of the creed. To summarize: "God" is an inclusive term which will admit the hyponym "father," in keeping with theology and tradition, but cannot *linguistically* accept femaleness.

E. Women Priests and Bishops

Not really so long ago — in 1896, to be exact — Pope Leo XIII, in his Bull *Apostolicae Curae*, declared Anglican orders null and void. Although it became incumbent upon Roman Catholics to accept this ruling, the declaration was issued from the Pope's lower magisterium and left open the possibility of change should later evidence warrant it. The Pope alleged that the Edwardian Ordinals of 1550 and 1552 had a defective intention — that is, that the Anglican Church did not *mean* what the Church had meant in past centuries when ordaining — and did not make unequivocally clear to which order, Bishop or Priest, a man was being ordained. Furthermore, the Pope argued, the ordinals did not mention the special "grace and power" of the particular order, namely, in the case of bishops, "the high-priesthood," and in the case of priests, "the power of consecrating and offering the true Body and Blood of our Lord" in the Eucharist, thus producing a "defect of form." Any open-minded person who has read *Apostolicae Curae* and then carefully examined the ordinals in question — reading *everything* including the prefaces — is led to agree with the conclusions reached by Dom Gregory Dix in his masterful study completed in 1956, *The Question of Anglican Orders*, that most Anglican ordinals, including the two Edwardian ones, are at least as good as their Roman counterparts.

For Roman Catholics, Leo's Bull settled things. For Anglicans, it meant the refusal or reluctance of Roman Catholics to participate in ecumenical affairs involving the Anglican Church. And that is the way things remained until the fresh air of Vatican II. Anglicans have always had self-doubt vis-a-vis the claims of Rome; Leo's Bull was cause for worry.

It was this same Pope Leo XIII who, on October 30, 1902, established the Pontifical Biblical Commission, the oldest of the formal commissions of the papacy in modern times. The purpose of the Commission was to regulate biblical interpretation and, at the same time, to promote biblical studies. Basically, it was conservative in its decrees. In the spring of 1976 the Commission took a vote on three matters concerning women in the priesthood. The first vote (17-0) revealed agreement that the New Testament does not settle the question whether women can be ordained priests. The second vote (12-5) asserted that, even if scriptural evidence indicated opposition to the ordination of women, that in itself would not be sufficient grounds for excluding women. The third vote (12-5) communicated the message that the Commission thought Christ's universal intention would not be thwarted if women were ordained. Rank confusion was introduced when church people realized there was a conflict between the findings of the Commission and the assertions contained in the Declaration issued by the Sacred Congregation for the Doctrine of the Faith. On January 27, 1977, the Declaration on the Question of the Admission of Women to the Ministerial Priesthood stated that "the church, in fidelity to the example of the Lord, does not consider herself authorized to admit women to priestly ordination." As support for excluding women from the priesthood, the Declaration called attention to the fact that Christ did not select any women as His Apostles, but that this should not be construed as evidence that He conformed to the customs of the times, for there were ample examples of His courage and independent action as well as of His admiration for and support of women. Nevertheless, the hermeneutic was that norms must be derived from historical facts, and Christ chose no women for His group. Just what authority the Declaration carried is not clear. What is clear is the continuing doubt in the Roman Church about the advisibility of ordaining women *from the historical point of view*.

Many Anglicans — men and women alike — share this uncertainty while admitting the fuzziness of scriptural evidence. For them and for the majority of Roman Catholics, most of the latter of whom by conscience adhere to the teachings of Rome — stated or implied — to admit women to the priesthood was to risk too much.

But what was the Episcopal Church risking by ordaining women? After all, Rome had rejected Anglican orders. Furthermore, why should Rome's approval be required for any step undertaken by another church?

The traditionalists offer two answers. First, in some sense, all Christian bodies are a part of the mind of Christ. Secondly, those bodies constructed and sustained on the foundation of the Apostolic Succession must inevitably look to each other for adherence to or deviation from that historical norm. The Anglican Church is a part of the Western Christian tradition and a Reformation offshoot of the Roman Church, like it or not. To strike out on one's own and/or to join with bodies for whom the Apostolic Succession is little more than an expression — at most a desirable attribute to which, conceivably, other denominations and sects might give allegiance — is an affront to the historic Catholic faith. Those who make such an assertion intend no affront to women; they readily admit the inconclusiveness of biblical evidence. However, on questions of such magnitude they insist upon cross-ecclesiastical consensus before decisive, non-reversible action is taken.

Why was this not done? There are at least three basic reasons, and not necessarily in this order. 1) Rome herself has consistently balked at the idea of ordaining women, for all the right or wrong reasons. Most have seemed to be based on the genuine conviction that Christ did not intend women to be priests; but some may have involved conserving the status quo, for after all, the Roman Church is largely a male preserve. 2) The Eastern Church has, by all her actions and pronouncements, characterized herself as rigid in such matters and has, in fact, cooperated markedly less in ecumenical areas than even Rome. 3) The Anglican Church — particularly that branch in the United States — sees herself as autonomous and quite capable of launching independent actions even of a profound nature. Apparently, it was not especially disturbing to the American Episcopal hierarchy to act counter to the mind of Canterbury and worldwide Anglicanism. The reasons for this super-independence lie in the attitudes of individual freedom germinated and nurtured in the 1960s. The specific impetus was feminism.

In 1974 eleven women, later known as the "Philadelphia Eleven," spurred by their great desire to become priests of the Episcopal Church and emboldened by the spirit of the times, were ordained in an irregular canonical fashion. That is, neither did they have the consent of the Bishop of Pennsylvania, in whose diocese the ordinations occurred, nor did their home diocesans approve the action. At first, the ordinations were dubbed invalid, but shortly most bishops agreed that they were probably valid. This was the crack in the door which has now swung wide open. Since 1976, when the ordination of women became legal, women have been becoming deacons and priests in record number all over the country. In 1989 the open door admitted the entrance of the first female bishop in the history of the Anglican Communion. That year marked the 200th anniversary of the Church's Constitution, establishing an ecclesiastical structure separate from that of the mother church in Great Britain. Article II, Section 2, of that Constitution, dealing with the consecration of bishops, makes no provision for the consecration of a woman. That this Article is not a piece of esoterica is attested to by the fact that the National Church, meeting in General Convention in Detroit, recommended, upon first presentation, that the Constitution be amended in order to permit the consecration of a woman. On February 11, 1989—after only a 4 1/2-month wait from her election on September 24, 1988—the Rev. Barbara C. Harris was consecrated Suffragan Bishop of Massachusetts despite the fact that the amendment will not, and cannot, become church law until it is adopted at the next General Convention in 1991. Two alternatives present themselves: either the Constitution has been nullified by this contemptuous action or Barbara Harris's consecration is null and void. Not a very pretty dilemma to be hung up on. But, as one parish priest said to the present writer, who, citing chapter and verse of canon law, had questioned his authority, and that of the licensing bishop, in granting permission to two Congregational ministers to pass the chalice: "Canon law is to be obeyed or ignored as circumstances dictate"—or words to that effect. The model of the clergy seems no longer to be the model of the church.

This last statement is confirmed in another way when we consider Barbara Harris's employment, educational, and pastoral background. A public relations executive for Sun Oil Company, a priest for only eight years, her work largely in association with the Episcopal Church Publishing Company (ECPC) except for part-time employment as a prison chaplain, she lacked the parish experience normally expected of someone elevated to the episcopate. After all, a bishop is supposed to be a "chief pastor."

She had only a high school education, no college degree, no seminary; she read for orders, a route thought closed for many years.

There were other objections. She was divorced. She was a rebel who joined with a group of bishops in 1974 in defying church law against ordaining women. As editor of the left-wing ECPC publication *The Witness*, she often fulminated against the "stupidity" of those who resisted any and all changes in the Episcopal Church. Her employment with ECPC reflects that organization's support of terrorism and totalitarianism and an admiration for Cuba and Nicaragua, two regimes not only violently hostile to the United States but sorely repressive of their own citizens.

Why in the name of all that is reasonable did the Diocese of Massachusetts pick a person of such a background to stand for election as a bishop? Harris was a woman, to be sure, but that was not enough. She had to be the sort of woman who would gain a hammerlock on the position. Her rebellious spirit—the reader is enjoined not to take that observation of an attribute as necessarily bad—coupled with her unconventional preparation and her color, assured her election, for it would be almost impossible to ignore, let alone unseat, such a combination for fear of being called illiberal and racist. Secondly, there is little doubt the Diocese of Massachusetts—or any diocese, for that matter—would not want to be the first to take a step that would be historic. A heavy burden of proof of the rightness of that step falls on the shoulders of the Diocese of Massachusetts, the National Church, and the person herself.

Despite the evidence or, as it were, the lack of evidence in scripture dealing with the ordination of women, we must try to discover the main objections held by many men, clerical and lay—and some women. It may be helpful to look at the recent history of the Episcopal Church with regard to women serving as deaconesses.

In 1853, a priest by the name of William Augustus Muhlenberg offered a memorial to the House of Bishops. In this memorial, among other objectives, was the suggestion that the bishops ordain — appoint or order would be more accurate — men for the purpose of supplementing the clerical outreach. They were to be authorized to use the Lord's Prayer, one of the creeds, the Gloria Patri, and certain other designated prayers in their conduct of Sunday services, and to adhere to the Prayer Book in the canon of the Eucharist. In short, they were to be layreaders of sort, yet ordained. The proposal met considerable resistance, particularly from the High Church faction, as might be expected, and ultimately failed of acceptance. Upon receiving the memorial, the House of Bishops appointed a committee headed by Bishop Alonzo Potter of Pennsylvania, who delivered an extensive analysis in 1857. Although the specifics of the memorial were let drop, numerous suggestions of a similar sort were issued by the committee. Among them was one for a ministry of women in some kind of sisterhood, a term resisted by many evangelicals as smacking of Romanism. For some years there had been agitation for the utilization of women's services in a more formal manner. The result was the establishment of the primitive order of deaconesses in 1889. There was objection from the Low Church element, but it shortly disappeared. The members of the order were to be unmarried women of good character over twenty-five years of age who were to work in a diocese only at the behest of the bishop.

For many years the role of deaconesses was debated. It centered about the question whether deaconesses were or were not in Holy Orders. As early as 1916 Archbishop William Temple declared his desire that women be ordained.

From 1920 on, the ordination of women—first as deaconesses, subsequently as priests—appeared on the agendas of Lambeth Conferences. In 1968 the Conference ruled that they were in Orders, and two years later the Episcopal Church agreed and changed its canons accordingly. But women never took to the order in any significant numbers, and today, to all intents and purposes, it is a dead issue and a defunct order.

Women have long constituted the largest congregational element of any church. Although some women today may, in retrospect, object to the ostensibly subordinate roles they have played in the life of the Church, they have served faithfully on altar guilds and in kitchens, have raised money, contributed money, taught Sunday School, and, with the advent of feminism, sought much more, but the question of Holy Orders loomed too large until recently. Now, as reported by the Association of Theological Schools in the U.S. and Canada and the National Council of Churches, they serve as ministers in eighty-four denominations. The mainline churches utilizing their services include the American Baptist, Episcopal, Evangelical Lutheran, Presbyterian, United Church of Christ, and the United Methodist. Their number exceeds 21,000 at the present. For the ten-year period 1977-1987, seminary graduates increased 224% (to 1,496). On the other hand, the number of male graduates increased by only 4.6% (to 5,394). Nearly one-third of all seminary students are now women. It will not be long before the women students will equal or exceed the number of men. According to Dean Otis Charles, the Episcopal Divinity School in Cambridge, Massachusetts, had 89 women enrolled as of the spring semester 1990. This figure represents 70% of their total enrollment.

From the standpoint of many men this fact constitutes a problem, for the number of available jobs for men is being reduced every day. In addition, there is a change in church atmosphere such that fewer men are enticed into attending worship services. They feel that the authority of the church has been diluted and that their own chances at leadership posts have been curtailed. The present writer has heard men — and occasionally women — comment, upon witnessing only women in the sanctuary, that "the whole picture is different." One man remarked, perhaps unfairly, "It sounds funny when she sings the Mass; her voice is so thin." Is this the grass roots talking? Should anybody be listening?

Most objections are more substantive and revolve about the image of Christ as the Ever-present Celebrant. Can a woman truly image Christ?

Another argument is, of course, tradition. Can the Church have been so wrong for nearly 2000 years as to limit the priesthood to males? What argument could be so compelling to cause us to break with that ancient tradition? Even the standard rejoinder that women represent half of humanity and offer complementary gifts to the Church is not totally convincing, for, it is argued, those gifts can be conveyed outside the priesthood. After all, most people — men and women alike — are not priests and yet make substantial contributions of talent to the Church, some, if not most — speaking strictly statistically — to a greater extent than the clergy. In fact, the argument goes on, it is hard to find a cleric today who differs markedly from the laity, so caught up is everybody in creature comforts, personal goals, and social and psychological problems. Why, the argument continues — perhaps on a pettier note — the divorce rate among the clergy is reflective of general society, and, in fact, a large number of women seeking or holding ordination seem to have been divorced. In fairness to such an observation, one must add that these critics are not making an incipient case for celibacy, but rather endorsing marital faithfulness.

For others — maybe for a majority of the disaffected — the ordination of women is just another change in a long list of worrisome innovations since the 1960s, even though many can see the logic in polity that allowed the consecration of a woman as bishop after the Church had permitted the ordination of women as deacons and priests. From the Prayer Book changes to the hassle over women priests to the pressure to ordain homosexuals to the unprecedented step of blessing out-of-wedlock arrangements to the marriage of homosexuals now being sought by some — it is all too much too fast. Where is the stability, the wisdom so sorely needed, asks the traditionalist?

Chapter III

The Problem: Its Effects

"Most religions do not make men better, only warier."

—*Elias Canetti*, Aufzeichnungen, *1952*

The effects of the changes in the Episcopal Church are manifold. They impinge not only directly upon the membership; they involve changed relations with constituents of the Anglican Communion as well as with other Catholic and Protestant bodies. Less important perhaps is the tacit stamp of approval the church puts upon contemporary American society. To some these changes are salutary; to others they are devastating; to still others they are a matter of the utmost indifference. Some reactions are based on reason and knowledge, some on ignorance. There is no excuse for indifference or ignorance.

One of the pragmatic effects is the startling loss of membership over the last twenty years. As reported in *Insight*, membership has plummeted from approximately 3.5 million in 1969 to 2.4 million in twenty years.[17] There is no doubt that some of this drop reflects the prevalent attrition in force among all mainline churches. Evidence in the form of membership in "splinter groups" and certain societies, such as the Prayer Book Society, reinforces the assumption that many Episcopalians have departed out of disgruntlement. In the *Church Annual* for 1989, the report of October 1, 1988 shows a loss of 42,207 members between 1986 and 1987.

It is possible to be philosophical about the matter. The Anglican Church has always been known as "the bridge church." To most, this moniker implied a bridge between the historic Catholic faith and evangelical

Christian expression, a healthy joining of two points of view. Few have thought that the bridge aspect of the church foretold the collapse of the bridge. As far as the Anglican Church in the United States is concerned, it does appear that a form of collapse is imminent. If it comes in the form of a union with COCU, it may not be seen as a collapse, which, from the standpoint of doctrine, it would be. We may prefer to call it an implosion or a cave-in. On the other hand, in fairness to the concept of a "bridge," we may simply reason that the *raison d'etre* of the Episcopal Church has been satisfied: The two sides have been brought together and thus the Episcopal Church can disappear from the scene.

A. The Success of Fundamentalism

Despite its pervasiveness on television throughout most of the 1970s and 1980s, fundamentalism as such was not new to America and probably did not require the extensive promotion it received. In fact, one could maintain today that, with a few notable exceptions, all that hype ultimately exposed the fraudulent aspects of fundamentalism and led to the downfall of a whole raft of televangelists.

America, as a frontier country, has always had its evangelistic side. The very notion of mass movement westward coincided with the itinerant nature and group appeal of the tent preachers. And the transplantation of all those people must have awakened in them the need for the stabilizing influence of religion.

What is wrong with that? Nothing.

Then, why look at the phenomenon of fundamentalism? Because it represents philosophically one opposite of liberalism even while its tent poles are sunk in the soil of the same religious certainty as the pillars of mainline liberal churches. The difference is that fundamentalism proclaims its sole reliance on the literal interpretation of the Bible—whatever that really means considering all the contradictions in scripture—while liberalism places its faith in a pragmatic view of the present.

Yet fundamentalism is a threat to the well-being of organized mainline churches, for, aside from a few "schisms," it knows what it is, where it is going, and how to get there. Its adherents must be located on or lean to the right; the subscribers to liberalism are seated to the left. Some in each group spend their time whacking away at the edges of the other, while those in the middle — dare we call them traditionalists? — float in the limbo of scripture tempered by tradition with cautious application to the present and future. Seen on a time line, fundamentalism is more regressive than "westward-moving," and liberalism is present- and future-oriented. The two expressions of faith seem to be headed in opposite directions like two planetary bodies repelling each other. The gravity that could bring them together is tradition.

The historical foundation of American fundamentalism can be found in a system of scriptural interpretation called dispensationalism. It originated in England and Ireland and arrived in North America in the 1850s. Probably, John Nelson Darby (1800-1882) devised the system. It was incorporated in the notes of the *Scofield Reference Bible* (1909), a work much beloved of fundamentalists.

Dispensationalism is hard to understand. Its basis is a series of God-delivered covenants to mankind in which God stipulates what it is that mankind must do to be saved. It is often possible to see these seven (or more) dispensations as marking significant epochs in history. For example, the church age in which we now live is a dispensation of the Holy Spirit which began at Pentecost and will end at Judgment Day with Christ's Second Coming. At His Second Coming certain things will happen; then other judgments will fall; the devil himself will be released to roam; and Christ will return once again to restore holy Israel upon earth. To verify all these steps requires close reading of scripture. Adherence to every jot and tittle is required. The system shares some aspects with general conservative Protestantism, but even the casual inquirer will recognize a distinctiveness that borders on the unique. That same inquirer will discern a latent distrust of modernism.

Fundamentalism is thus a movement that took its cue from literalism. It arose early in the twentieth century among conservative members of various Protestant denominations, but did not acquire a name until 1920 when Curtis Lee Laws, editor of *The Watchman-Examiner*, a Baptist paper, used the term to describe "those ready to do battle royal for the Fundamentals." By "fundamentals" he meant the Virgin Birth, the bodily Resurrection of Christ, the substitutional atonement, the absolute infallibility of the Bible, and the physical Second Coming of Christ. Among the denominations immediately and deeply attracted by this theology were the Baptists and the Presbyterians.

It was easy to recognize in the movement a reaction to liberal theological attempts to make Christianity fit the scientific and historic thought of the times. The controversy climaxed publicly in the famous Scopes "monkey trial." (Compare the flap in the 1980s over "creationism" in the schools.)

As is well known, William Jennings Bryan prosecuted the case, and Clarence Darrow served as defense attorney. Despite Bryan's claim that he was an expert in biblical matters, Darrow made a fool of him before a huge crowd. However, since it had been obvious to all from the start, including Darrow, that everybody was seeking a guilty verdict, Darrow hinted that he would accept that verdict and continue to work on Scopes's behalf on appeal. The judge expunged the Darrow-Bryan debate from the court record and summoned the jury. They found Scopes guilty of teaching evolution to school children, and the judge fined him $100. However, the matter did not end there. Upon appeal, the Tennessee Supreme Court ruled that the judge had committed an error in levying the fine whereupon, at the suggestion of the court, the prosecution nol-prossed the case.

What had seemed to be an initial victory against the teaching of evolution in the schools was, therefore, short-lived, and fundamentalists began to regroup into splinter sects under the general mantle of "old-time religion." Most of these sects were of the "Holiness" and "Pentecostal" sort. The Methodists, Presbyterians, Congregationalists, and others had begun to de-emphasize the revivalist aspects of their religious expression. This action was seen by the fundamentalists as dangerous to the discovery of religious truth. In addition, they saw such "standard" denominations as fouled by a strong intinction of biblical criticism and the hated social gospel. By the middle of the century a division into "pure fundamentalists" and "evangelicals" became evident. Of the first group, such leaders as Bob Jones, Carl McIntire, and John R. Rice continued militant activity. They were followed by Oral Roberts, Pat Robertson, Jimmy Swaggart, Jim Bakker, and the more moderate Robert Schuyler and Jerry Falwell. Billy Graham was, and remains, the archetypal representative of the evangelicals.

Fundamentalism, evangelicalism — call it what you will — is alive and well in the United States. It is functioning well because its appeal has grown and a wide coalition has been established across denominational lines reminiscent of the early part of the century. Where Oral Roberts or Jimmy Swaggart fails (or failed in the case of defrocking or demise) to attract a following, there always remains someone of only slightly different stripe. The result has been that even members of the same church can have as their second pastor one or more of the "superpastors" of television. Those that are officially unchurched can, of course, ally themselves directly with one or more of the TV churches. It hardly needs saying that this step often spells the financial undoing of the vulnerable in the television audience.

In the 1950s, when the call for money was muted, the best-known of the radio and TV figures were Norman Vincent Peale, the Methodist-turned-Reform pastor of New York City's Marble Collegiate Church, and Monsignor Fulton J. Sheen, professor of theology on the faculty of the Catholic University of America in Washington, D.C. These two were able to speak simply and convincingly to millions of people. They received almost universal praise for eloquence. If they were the distillate of American frontier religion, they were hard to recognize. Billy Graham, on the other hand, who has shared the same widespread respect for his simplicity and honesty in presenting the Christian religion to mass audiences, is, from the standpoint of his unabashed Calvinism—that only God can save the sinner; the sinner cannot do it on his own—more clearly a continuation of that revival tradition of which we have spoken.

What can we make of this phenomenon of mass appeal?

One answer is that somebody—even very large numbers of people—will buy anything. No disrespect toward any denomination is intended by making such an assertion. We have only to witness the selling of the Communist ideology or the phenomenon of Hitler's rise and maintenance of power to understand what is meant. Who can forget the rallies in Munich, Nuremberg, Berlin, and elsewhere and the hypnotic commitment they induced? Anything said often enough, loudly enough, and long enough has a good chance of being believed. If an element of crisis can be injected into the message, the result will be forthcoming sooner. Fundamentalist messages are of the crisis sort: Jesus Saves (you must come to Jesus; you can't save yourself); the devil will get you (if you do this or that); the Bible says you must tithe (if you don't, this crusade/enterprise will go under). It is an effective strategy.

Why is it that no single brand of religion can succeed on the same scale? Even Monsignor Sheen's "Catholic Hour," backed by the world's largest denomination, couldn't sell Catholicism so much as Christianity. Why did not millions unconsciously, subliminally, devise the formula "Christianity = Catholicism"? Perhaps because selling religion in America is like selling any other product: one can develop brand loyalty only so far. Then somebody makes a better product, and then somebody else makes a better one yet. (Or, at least that is the perception.) By now these products have become a generic commodity, and the brand doesn't matter. You never hear a televangelist advertize his own denomination.

Where, then, does the secret lie? Why, until recently, have the fundamentalists been so successful in gaining membership for their particular enterprises, restoring membership in sister churches, sharing membership with sister churches, and raising huge amounts of money? First and foremost, they have a message that sells, and they sell the message in the good old American business way through the favorite media—TV and radio—and with all the glitz and personality worship that Americans have come to love and require. Secondly, they have joined religion with social issues—shades of the social gospel! If you are a fundamentalist, you are a member of the "moral majority." The political power of such a group is often awesome.

One question remains. *Why* does the message of the fundamentalists sell, but not that of the Episcopalians? Because, basically, the former know who they are, what they want, and where they are headed. Everybody wants to buy a sure thing; nobody wants to buy uncertainty, confusion, maudlin compromise. Of course, selling a message is no proof of the truth of the message — *caveat emptor*! But, then, neither is not selling a message proof of its falsity.

It would be unfair to blame fundamentalism in any of its manifestations directly for the decline of membership in the more moderate mainline churches. For one thing, we know that fundamentalist ideas, often accessed through the visual medium of television, have buttressed some faltering denominations. For good or for bad, there is evidence of fundamentalist philosophical influence in the spread of the charismatic movement even within the Episcopal and Roman Churches.

It can also be shown that certain aspects of a return to a "roots" religion can be attributed to a growing fundamentalist atmosphere. It is not unfair, though, to censure mainline churches for not providing on their own the means of satisfaction of their membership. This does not necessarily mean underwriting fundamentalist doctrine, especially if that doctrine does violence to existing beliefs. What it means is, rather, restating or reinterpreting beliefs in such a convincing, sure way that there is no need to look elsewhere for the comfort and certainty to which a believer should be entitled. The reinterpretation does not rest upon any pandering to the times, but involves the assurance that the church in question, being also an object of God's concern, contains sufficient validity to stand on its own. That "arsenal" in the Episcopal Church to which Billy Sunday alluded contains not only ammunition to defend against the attacking nether forces but also weapons of benign aggression for the promulgation of its views. The Baptists do not apologize for their autonomous congregational attitudes, nor for their internal splits, nor for their self-imposed exclusion from many joint church endeavors on the national and international scene. The appeal of the Southern Baptist Church alone has been enormous in the last two decades, even in the Soviet Union. The Mormons, hardly a "conventional" church, happily go their own way—and add members by the thousands every year. The Orthodox and Eastern Rite Churches chug along unwaveringly.

The recent steps of Prayer Book revision and the ordination of women in the Episcopal Church were the result as much of the Church's lack of sure identity as of the Church's liberal stance. Was the Church's action suicidal, or was it a feat of self-sacrifice to the greater good? Was it calculated to advance members of the hierarchy by giving them greater influence in a larger organization and control over larger numbers of people? These are impertinent questions, but many people are asking them.

B. No Place To Go

There stood the little girl, all decked out in her Sunday-go-to-meetin' dress. Suddenly, there was a knock at the door, and a man's voice was heard to say to her parents, "I'm sorry to tell you, but there won't be any church for a long time. The building burned down last night."

"What am I going to do?" wailed the little girl. "I won't see all my friends in church. I'm all dressed up, with nowhere to go!"

Superficial? Maybe.

A teenaged boy and his parents were in the midst of an argument.

"You're *not* going back to that church again, and that's final!" ordered the father.

"Why? Just tell me why!" yelled the boy.

"Because we are not going to have you subjected to all the misinformation they're putting out."

"But I'm old enough to decide that for myself," insisted the youngster.

"Not while you are living at home," retorted the mother.

Unlikely situation? Unreasonable parental response? Perhaps.

An older married couple were in conversation. They had spent a lifetime in their church, raised their children there, served on the vestry, contributed many thousands of dollars. Now they have stopped pledging and have scarcely entered a church in two years.

"You know, what I don't understand is why no member of the clergy has called to inquire why we don't come to church anymore," began the wife. "They are quick to go to the hospital when you're physically sick."

"What I don't understand is why no one is willing to talk openly and carefully about the serious issues facing the Church. I thought the Episcopal Church was supposed to be so liberal. Why won't the Church listen to both sides, to people like us?" asked the husband.

"They don't care, that's why," said the wife.

Improbable conversation? Not on your life.

These fictitious mini-dramatizations lay bare some of the many problems associated with recent controversial actions by the Episcopal Church. There are tens of thousands of real people who have no spiritual refuge today. To less complex minds, the Church has been burnt down, destroyed, to arise in an entirely different form. To others, for whom the Church had represented a safe buffer for their children against the errancy of society, the Church's teachings have become suspect. There is also that collection of dedicated Churchmen and -women who are disaffected. They simply cannot understand why their Church does not minister to them in their present emotional state the way it does when they are physically ill. Their conclusion is that the Church will not do so because either it does not want to face up to its mistakes, or it does not know how, or it is so certain of its actions that it will not question them, or it hopes that time will cause the problems to go away.

Consider some of the options open to the disaffected:

1. *Stay in the Church and do battle for what you believe.*

How many times have Episcopalians heard this? Too many to count. For many war-weary members it is too much to ask after a quarter century of turmoil. Scarcely ever is a battle won—and when it seems to be, fresh attacks overwhelm the defenders until victory is turned into defeat. These people have lost their spirit and their commitment to their Church. They can no longer rationalize the Church's position on so many issues.

2. *Work outside the Church as well in order to effect the needed changes within.*

Speak to other churches about your stance on issues. Write about it. Join groups peripherally connected with the Church whose objectives coincide with your own. Many do all these things; some report they feel too deflated to try.

3. *Join another Episcopal parish.*

Maybe the clergy there will be resistant enough to the innovations that you can survive with a minimum of rationalization.

4. *Join one of the breakaway Episcopal groups.*

That is, if you don't mind trading your long-time church home—buildings do matter—for the Sunday use of some school auditorium.

5. *Stay home and pray about it.*

This was the advice given by a priest friend and former colleague — a prescription easier to deliver than for a layman to keep.

6. *Join the Roman Church.*

For most, the reasons for not being Roman in the first place have not changed, although for many such a step is becoming much more likely.

7. *Join the Orthodox Church.*

This is hard to do if one is not conveniently of some ethnic background.

8. *Join a Protestant church that seems to offer the fewest doctrinal differences from your own faith.*

The main reasons for not being a Protestant persist anyhow and make this an especially difficult option. Wouldn't it be easier to stay in the Episcopal Church with half a pie until it becomes Protestant under COCU? At least, you would have been beside its deathbed.

9. *Forget the Church and its problems and live without the stress.* (After all, you knew the Church was going to do itself in; you saw it coming years ago.)

How does one do that after a lifetime in the Church?

Is any one of these options viable? Is there a magical combination? Before we search for solutions in the final chapter, some more history is in order.

CHAPTER IV

The Backdrop of Church History

"But one thing is perfectly plain — whether or not liberals are Christians, it is at any rate perfectly clear that liberalism is not Christianity."

—*J. Gresham Machen,* Christianity and Liberalism, *1923*

Church history is history pure and simple. Christianity is founded upon historical fact. Jesus, a Jew, was born in Bethlehem, raised in Nazareth, lived and preached throughout Galilee and Judea, and died in Jerusalem. In a direct sense, Christianity is an offshoot of Judaism; Jesus's followers believed that He fulfilled the Old Testament prophecies of the long-awaited Messiah. The central teachings of the Christian religion maintain that Jesus is the Son of God, the second person of the Trinity of God the Father, God the Son, and God the Holy Ghost; that Jesus's earthly life, his death, resurrection, and ascension prove that God loves humankind and is willing to forgive all manner of sin; and that faith in Jesus Christ is sufficient to achieve salvation and eternal life. These tenets are enshrined in the Bible and interpreted by tradition.

Jesus Himself was aware of his mission from boyhood, though his active ministry extended a scant three years. He once asked his disciple Peter, "Who do men say that I am?" Peter answered, "Thou art the Christ." By that he surely meant the Messiah, the anointed one, who had been promised the Jews in the Old Testament.

Jesus did not depart from history upon his crucifixion by the Romans at Jerusalem between 29 and 33 A.D., for His followers were certain, and countless millions since believe that he actually rose from the dead and ascended into heaven. He had always lived as part of the Trinity; He returned to that supernatural state while simultaneously existing among people on earth. Christianity thus resembles a mixture of Platonism and Aristotelianism in proclaiming an unending time process, and Judaism in recognizing "God's mighty acts" of intervention in the lives of humans.

Christianity is a way of life through history and beyond. Here on earth the new life was to be based on the love of one's neighbor, on the establishment of the community. The life hereafter was to reflect a "communion of saints."

This idea of timelessness punctuated by significant events is worth keeping in mind. There is a hint of the identity of timelessness with tradition.

1. Of Rome

One of the truly great epics of history is the story of Rome, its development from an insignificant pastoral settlement into one of the world's greatest cultural, intellectual, and religious centers. Its age, continuity, complexity, and organization have rightfully earned it the name "The Eternal City." Chief city of the world's most durable empire, city of law, city of beauty, Rome has left a bold and deep imprint on western civilization.

It was no mean advantage to the Faith that Rome early became the focal point of Christianity. Around 100 A.D., in a letter to the church at Smyrna, St. Ignatius of Antioch proclaimed, "Wherever Jesus Christ is, there also is the Catholic Church." It is not altogether clear whether he merely meant that Christ stands at the center of the catholic, or universal, church or whether his designation had some special significance for Rome. The Church has historically chosen the latter possibility because Ignatius was the first in Christian literature to use the term "Catholic" and to teach that the only guarantee against heresy is a church united under a bishop. In his letter to the Ephesians, he wrote, "We ought to look upon the bishop even as we would upon the Lord Himself." When one considers Christ's statement that He would found His Church upon Peter, the Rock (Matt. 16:18), it is not difficult to see how the idea of a succession of bishops was established in view of Peter's status as the first bishop of Rome and how he might attain the supreme authority among the apostles.

A. The Claims of the Roman Church

The first, and fundamental, claim of the Roman Church from the standpoint of organization was, therefore, based on Peter's primacy among the apostles. When this contention was added to the Church's assertion that it was the Catholic and universal church within Christendom, it was natural that Peter's successors could claim to have inherited Peter's authority. In effect, this meant that that authority was divine in origin, because it came directly from Christ Himself, and that Peter and his successors, later known as popes, were the rightful dispensers of church law and the sacraments. With such divine authority the Church has always felt it could demand obedience from its adherents and proclaim unity in faith and doctrine. The Church rests its case on the complete passage from Matthew, a portion of which was referred to above: (Matt. 16:17-19) "And Jesus answered and said unto him, Blessed art thou, Simon Bar-jona: for flesh and blood hath not revealed it unto thee, but my Father which is in heaven. And I say also unto thee, That thou art Peter, and upon this rock I will build my church; and the gates of hell shall not prevail against it. And I will give unto thee the keys of the kingdom of heaven: and whatsoever thou shalt bind on earth shall be bound in heaven: and whatsoever thou shalt loose on earth shall be loosed in heaven." The Church interprets the last part to mean that Peter — and his successors, and their representatives, the priests — have the divine authority to forgive, or not to forgive, people's sins, thereby establishing the sacrament of Penance.

There follows from this principle of authority that the Church, being a divine institution guided by Christ from its inception through the present, cannot err, for God would not have established His Church and then allowed it to fall into error. Its primary teachers, the popes, are partners to divine revelation and are therefore infallible in their pronouncements on faith and morals.

Although this has been a belief of the Church since earliest times, the dogma of papal infallibility was not enunciated until 1870, by the First Vatican Council. The dogma is very specific. The Pope does not err in matters of faith and morals when speaking *ex cathedra*, that is, from the chair of Peter, as the visible head of the Church. In addition, when an ecumenical council makes definitive pronouncements that are ratified by the Pope, they too are considered infallible. The scriptural warrant for this dogma is found in John 14:16,17, where Jesus speaks: "And I will pray the Father, and he shall give you another Comforter, that he may abide with you for ever; Even the Spirit of truth; whom the world cannot receive, because it seeth him not, neither knoweth him: but ye know him; for he dwelleth with you, and shall be in you."

The question may be asked: Does papal infallibility rule out inerrancy of the Bible? The Roman Church takes the position that the Bible is the inspired word of God, that it contains truth for all people in all times, but that the Church has, within its scope of tradition, the sole right to interpret holy scripture, and the Church will not err in doing so. It is certainly historically correct to maintain that the Church existed before the New Testament and that it was the Church that selected, recognized, and arranged the books of the entire Bible. Thus, the Church looks upon the Bible always in tandem with tradition.

The authority of tradition has also been the basis for such other major dogmas as those touching upon the veneration of saints — especially the Virgin Mary — relics, images, and purgatory, for the Church claims no scriptural warrant for these in the Bible. The veneration of Mary, mother of Jesus, goes back to a very early stage of the Church. So exalted a person was she, she must have aroused considerable curiosity, respect, love, and trust in the people, so that within a relatively short time she began to be regarded as sinless from the start. That is to say, from her very conception she had been preserved from every taint of original sin. This dogma of the Immaculate Conception, in all respects a confirmation of the implicit belief of the Church all along, was defined in 1854 by Pope Pius IX, making acceptance of it, as in the case of all dogmas, necessary for salvation. Not only the Roman Church, but also the Orthodox and Anglican Churches proclaim and teach the perpetual virginity of Mary.

In 1950 Pope Pius XII defined and proclaimed the Assumption of Mary. Upon her death her body was miraculously saved from corruption, resurrected, and taken up into heaven. This, too, had been a pious belief of the Church for many hundreds of years.

Another belief hallowed by years of acceptance is that of purgatory. Even the ancient Jews prayed for the dead; it was natural that Christians should continue to do so. The likelihood of some middle state between earth and heaven has struck all Christians as eminently logical, for we would not be able to tolerate the vision of God in our imperfect state. That state would include the overlay of venial — that is, minor — sins upon our conscience. We must be purged — thus, purgatory — of these sins before we can enter into the fullness of heaven. The prayers of the Church militant — the Church on earth — can be efficacious.

It can be concluded from the above claims and their bases that the Roman Church gives to its hierarchy the right to rule over and to decide for its members many matters of belief. Judging from one of the sentences addressed to popes upon their enthronement, it could be maintained that the power of the hierarchy extends even further: "Know thyself to be the Ruler of the World, the Father of princes and kings, and the earthly Vicar of Jesus Christ our Savior."

B. Protestant Counter-Claims

To speak of counter-claims implies an adversarial attitude on the part of Protestants toward Roman Catholics. It would be unfortunate to allow such an impression to stand. Although there are militantly anti-Catholic Protestant bodies and individuals, and although there are negative attitudes and actions that emanate from the Roman Catholic Church, the fact is, these two branches of the same religion profess similar basic beliefs and often learn from and share with each other. It is precisely in the area of *claims* made by the Roman Church that Protestants — and here are meant all non-Roman churches except the Orthodox — become resistant, for most Protestant churches do not have a hierarchical structure that promulgates dogma and simply cannot comprehend such a regulatory body. It is, therefore, in the very definition of "church" that Protestants part company with Rome.

In case the word "Protestant" connotes a certain belligerency, it should be explained that Protestants consider themselves "affirmers" more than "protestors." The term derives from the *Protestatio* issued by a minority of delegates in 1529 against the Diet of Speyer for having denied them their freedom to obey the Word of

God. For three years they had been permitted to make Luther's evangelical Christianity the official religion of their states. Then they were suddenly told there would be no further "religious innovations." Since the controversy over freedom within religion arose at the time of the Reformation, when all of Rome's excesses were caught in a bright light, it is easy to see how the animosity toward Rome has persisted all these centuries. What an irony that the only non-Roman church to use "Protestant" in its name, a church more clearly Catholic than any other, was the Episcopal Church, who prefixed it in 1783 and retained it — often under considerable "protest"! — for nearly two hundred years.

But what do Protestants see as wrong about a hierarchical church that seems to limit freedom within religion by interpreting scripture and tradition for its people? First, they maintain all religious truth is enshrined in the Bible and every person can interpret it for him- or herself. Secondly, they accept no infallible statements by the popes; the latter, like other humans, have often been wrong.

Except for Episcopalians and Swedish Lutherans, Protestants reject the basis of Rome's claim to superiority. They insist that the authority Jesus gave Peter — "the keys of the kingdom" — was not administrative and was not to be passed on in any kind of apostolic succession. As for papal infallibility — and here the Episcopalians and Swedish Lutherans rejoin the group — it is condemned as without foundation in scripture and is considered by most as not replacing conciliar decisions and even as incompatible with the headship of Christ. For most Protestants — and here it is difficult to know whom to subtract, if anybody — the Church is primarily a fellowship of believers, permeated by the Holy Spirit, who look to Christ as leader. The problem has been to hear Christ's directions in any uniform way. The result has been a huge variety of Protestant denominations, particularly in the

United States, where the count is even controversial, extending from a low of 200 to over 250. Some of this variety can certainly be attributed to vitality, but more can probably be blamed on narrowness and self-assertion.

In the area of salvation most Protestants are uncomfortable that it should be conditional upon merit. The Roman Church maintains that salvation is by grace alone and not by man's efforts, but Protestants feel that nevertheless the Church often links merit with grace when it describes the latter as a gift from God which makes humankind worthy of salvation. Again, all but Episcopalians and Swedish Lutherans, both of whom base the efficacy of their priests' actions upon the transmitted authority from the Apostles, resist the notion that there are intermediaries between God and man whose actions are the bearers of grace.

Coupled with the idea of merit, as seen by some Protestants, is the veneration of saints. Most Protestants — we can exclude Episcopalians here at least on some occasions — object to praying to saints for the reason that doing so tends to devalue the sovereignty of God. If God is all-merciful, then He is accessible to all under all circumstances. For most Protestants, Mary is just another saint whose intercessory powers are not required to reach God.

Intercession plays a vital part in the release of souls from purgatory, a theory rejected by most Protestant denominations. For them, perhaps the most disturbing feature is that the Roman Church attempts to control the destiny of souls even after death, for it claims to be able to remit the temporal punishment due to sins and therefore to shorten or eliminate the time spent in purgatory.

All Protestant objections are clearly based on rejection of the authority Rome has aggregated unto herself, and this includes, except for Episcopalians and the Swedish Lutherans, even Apostolic Succession. If the authority were recognized, the doctrines that follow from it could be more easily accepted. But, from the standpoint of "pure" Protestantism, if any piece of that authority remains, it must be eliminated. By having insisted upon Apostolic Succession as necessary to the Church, the Episcopal Church put itself in jeopardy by linking up with the myriad Protestant denominations and sects. Church authority is anathema to Protestants; their task has been to remake the Anglican Communion. They have been remarkably successful.

2. Of the East

Like Protestants, the Orthodox reject Rome's claim to a superior position among Christian bodies. Their rejection includes the notion of a single individual, a pope, as head of the earthly church. For the Orthodox, the pope is historically one of the five patriarchs. His position was, and is, coequal with that of any of the other four. Infallibility does not rest with the pope, nor with any other patriarch.

Up to the time the Emperor Constantine relocated his capital from Rome to Constantinople in 330 A.D., the Church had been one. In the West, Rome was the only patriarchate; in the East, there were four: Constantinople, Alexandria, Antioch, and Jerusalem. All agreed on most essentials: the apostolic succession, the Nicene Creed, and the seven sacraments.

Although the effect of Constantine's move east was largely political and produced the first gulf between the Church of the West and the Church of the East, there were also major linguistic and philosophical differences between the churches that made the split less surprising upon reflection. The language of the West was Latin; of the East, Greek. Organizationally, the Roman Church sought to bring everyone under its direct control; to assist in this objective it insisted upon the use of the Latin language. The Orthodox Church, however, tended from the start to divide into independent national and social groups. This first division of the Church was more geographical and political than anything else.

The tension between East and West did not abate. Occupied for several hundred years in containing the Gothic threat and in quelling uprisings throughout western Europe, Roman legions were often hard-pressed. It was not until the reign of Pope Leo III, who was threatened with deposition by the Romans, that the picture began to change. For many years Charlemagne had been invading countries, fighting Muslims, forcing conversions to Christianity, carrying out massacres, and subjugating peoples. Knowing Charlemagne's loyalty to the faith, Pope Leo appealed to him to come to Rome in 799 to lend his support. Charlemagne consented immediately. On Christmas Day of the year 800 Charlemagne was crowned Holy Roman Emperor by the pope, thus making the Roman Church conterminous with the Holy Roman Empire. This coronation widened the gap between the Byzantine and Roman empires.

More widening occurred when, in 857, Ignatius in Constantinople would not administer communion to Caesar Bardas because of his demonstrated immorality. From this incident arose a squabble which resulted in Ignatius's being forced from the patriarchate. A Greek lay churchman and theologian by the name of Photius was chosen to fill his place. A fast shuffle took place, and within one week he had been ordained priest and consecrated a bishop. This was hardly canonical, but the legates from Rome actually accepted the procedure. The problem came from Pope Nicholas I, who refused to recognize Photius. Despite the papal objection, Photius was installed. He began immediately to criticize the pope for various actions. His most virulent attack centered on Rome's insertion of the infamous *filioque* clause in the

Nicene Creed which proclaimed that the Holy Spirit emanated not only from the Father but also from the Son. From this point, Ignatius and Photius played musical chairs with the patriarchate, with Photius stepping down and then reassuming the patriarchate upon Ignatius's death. Nicholas, who had since died, was succeeded by Pope John VIII, who recognized Photius's election as legitimate. Many years later the controversy over Photius and his resistance to the *filioque* clause were seen as instrumental in creating the schism between East and West in the 11th century.

Pope St. Leo IX lived only 52 years, from 1002 to 1054, and was Pope for only five years, from 1049 to 1054. But he lived a very full and important life, indeed. As pope he traveled far and wide and attacked clerical excesses wherever he found them. He was particularly assiduous in his fight against simony. He waded into the conflict between Berengar of Tours and Lanfranc over the Real Presence in the Eucharist. He did true diplomatic service among quarreling nations. He increased the Roman Church's land holdings. He engaged in war with the Normans in south Italy, but lost. But he will be remembered most of all for his having excommunicated, in 1054, Michael Cerularius, the patriarch of Constantinople, and all his adherents, so rankled was the pope by the patriarch's bitter attack against him. Constantinople obliged by excommunicating Rome. The schism became final four hundred years later and has never been repaired.

The Isolation and Ethnic Exclusivity of the Orthodox Church

The perception of the Orthodox Church as an isolated and ethnically exclusive body is present largely in that area where the membership is less numerous, namely, in the West. In the United States, for example, there are perhaps no more than 3,000,000 Orthodox church members, a figure, incidentally, that is actually higher than the number of Episcopalians. Not counted here are the members of the five Eastern (non-Roman) Rite Churches, for example, the Maronites and Melchites, all of whom bear allegiance to the pope even though their liturgies are Orthodox.

There are problems with this figure, as with all church statistics. Some churches count all baptized members; some count only communicants; some count baptized or confirmed members in good standing. Among the Orthodox it is typical to base the count on baptismal records. Since infants are confirmed immediately after being baptized, there is no further effect on the statistic. But sometimes parish statistics are given, in which case the count involves only male communicants over the age of 21.

In addition to the four ancient patriarchates of Constantinople, Alexandria, Antioch, and Jerusalem, there are also the patriarchates of Romania, Bulgaria, Serbia, and the Soviet Union (Russia and Georgia). The Orthodox churches of Greece, Albania, Poland, Finland, Czechoslovakia, and Cyprus possess autonomous national status. In the United States most of these churches are under the supervision of archbishops of their respective nationalities. It can readily be seen that this mishmash of language, culture, and control renders orthodoxy generally inaccessible to persons who are not naturally a part of a given culture. Orthodox churches are also typically confined to large urban areas where immigrants from these countries reside together in large numbers. Most people in the United States can live a lifetime and never encounter an Orthodox Christian. Such a situation virtually excludes Orthodoxy as a viable option for persons dissatisfied with their own brand of Christianity.

This is unfortunate, for the Orthodox Church can be considered a bridge church in many of the same respects as the Anglican Church. Not only does Orthodoxy not recognize the primacy and infallibility of the pope, its doctrine, like that of Protestantism, is based on the Bible. The Church preserves holy tradition and the decrees of the seven ecumenical councils: two at Nicea, three at Constantinople, one at Ephesus, and one at Chalcedon. Its government is episcopal, and there is usually a council consisting of bishops, priests, and laymen. A synod of bishops is presided over by an elected patriarch, metropolitan, or archbishop. The ministry is the familiar threefold one of bishops, priests, and deacons. A priest may marry before he is ordained, but not thereafter — not even if his wife should die. Bishops are chosen from among the monastic communities and, of course, are celibate.

To the casual visitor to an Orthodox service, the ritual observed seems to exclude all but the completely initiated. Elaborate, prolonged, with much coming and going, frequent responses, much crossing of oneself, some action behind the iconostasis, considerable intoning of prayers, usually in a foreign language, the liturgy is framed in a church filled with holy pictures and other unrecognizable paraphernalia. Frank Stanton Burns Gavin (1890-1938) has said it in a slightly different way: "In the details of Eastern worship is a rough epitome of the history of Eastern Christendom: the *ikons*, about which a bitter controversy once raged; the service in the vernacular as against Latin; the existence of both a married and a celibate priesthood; the strong and passionate loyalty to the national allegiance evidenced by the provision of special prayers for the rulers by name — all these mark the characteristics, peculiarities, and contrasts with the customs of the West."[18] Coupled with these unfamiliar aspects of worship is a theology that many in the West — including Roman Catholics — consider unusually rigid. It is little wonder that outsiders do not seek to join Orthodox churches.

3. Effects of the Reformation

It would be presumptuous to pretend that the Reformation in its myriad aspects can be neatly analyzed, so complex was the movement. To assign dates of its appearance and disappearance within the 16th century is to treat the upheaval as merely a synchronic phenomenon. To assume that it was no more than an attempt to reform the Roman Catholic Church, which resulted in the creation of the Protestant Church, overlooks the political and economic factors at play. There is, in short, no pocket-dictionary definition.

An examination of the roster of participants yields information about the movement's genesis, its pervading spirit, and its achievements. For centuries opponents of orthodox views had periodically asserted themselves, and as early as the 14th century John Wyclif headed up a dissident movement that was continued by Jan Huss in Bohemia in the following century. For his resistance to Catholicism, Huss was burned at the stake in 1415 by order of the Council of Constance. His demise led directly to a series of bloody encounters in the 15th century called the Hussite Wars. What had begun as a religious struggle against the Church evolved into a national battle between Czechs and Germans and a social conflict between the peasants and the gentry. Eventually, compromises were arrived at in the secular sphere, but the challenge to orthodoxy persisted. People saw more and more clearly what monstrous abuses the Church had sanctioned or ignored and demanded reform in the personal lives of the clergy and in the doctrines they espoused, some of which, like simony, exacted the economic ruin of the common people. One of the healthy results of this grass roots criticism was a concerted attempt to reestablish the ecumenical council, rather than the pope, as the supreme lawgiving body of the Church. Even though the movement came to nought, the spirit of reform was strengthened.

And it never lost its momentum, thanks to such Renaissance humanists as Desiderius Erasmus, Lorenzo Valla, Johann Reuchlin, Ulrich von Hutten, and Philip Melanchthon. All these men, and Zwingli and Calvin too, discovered their weapons of attack against the organized Church in the study of the classics, ancient languages, and the Bible. This new critical attitude transformed the notion of the people as a faceless mob into the idea that they were distinct individuals. The confidence that was engendered contributed to the development of strong cities and nations that were ready to assert themselves against the powers of Rome, both secular and spiritual. The invention of printing hastened the advent of the Reformation and accelerated the distribution of the ideas of the movement. The scene was well set for the sudden appearance of a hitherto unknown professor of theology at Wittenberg University, Martin Luther.

The university, one of nine in Germany alone founded between 1456 and 1506 — clear evidence of a Renaissance-inspired intellectual awakening — was a mere fifteen years old in 1517 when Luther nailed his famous 95 Theses to the front door of the Schlosskirche in defiance of Pope Leo X and his granting of well-paying indulgences. This action signaled the historical start of the Reformation and set the tone for all the daring deeds and thought to follow.

Luther himself was a curious combination of scholar and pragmatist. To be sure, he was no great theologian, but he had an orderly mind. He was convinced Rome was theologically wrong in the matter of indulgences, and by design or not, he knew how to anger the hierarchy. He also knew how to enlist the anger of the people against the hierarchy. When, in 1520, he burned the papal bull issued against him by Leo, the crowd surrounding him outside the Elster Gate in Wittenberg was enormous. Fundamental to his thinking and his actions was the idea of Christian liberty, of the freedom of the individual from the bondage of institutions, even the institution of the Church. For Luther, no matter how much good inheres in the Church, the individual person has equal value before God, to Whom he or she has direct access without the filter of the Church. This means that every person has the right to criticize the institution — even to eschew it — as long as everybody will answer to his own conscience. Institutions — even the Church — are made up of people who sometimes turn corrupt. It is, therefore, the duty of people at large to remake any institution that gives evidence of gross sinfulness, no matter how sacred that institution may be. Furthermore, much doubt attaches to the notion that somehow the clergy are more special than any of the other people.

Religion, then, is not merely a matter of the Church; it is a matter of the people.

These principles of individual freedom of thought and action and the deinstitutionalizing of the Church became threads linking the now-defunct medieval world with the emerging modern period. The implementation of these principles depended upon the education of the people, an ideal long expressed by the Church in the hope that the people could better understand doctrine. It was, however, an ideal not really believed by the people and, as many maintained, not really sought with great vigor by the Church. In his many tracts, letters, and public addresses — it is said he wrote a book every two weeks, over a hundred volumes in his lifetime — Luther was consistent in his stressing of the need for education for young and old, rich and poor, noble and common. To this end he translated first the Greek New Testament and, later, the whole Bible into German so that it might be personally comprehended.

Although others espoused his views, no one did so with the same courage and conviction as Luther. The combination of his peasant background and his innate intelligence refined by his theological training in the Church produced the irony of the enemy within serving the needs of those suspicious of their holy institution. His brashness and crudity—he could hurl epithets with the best of them—joined with an odd spiritual depth to form a winning combination among the masses. He was the embodiment of the tension within the Catholic Church and that between the Church and society. That tension was further exhibited in the concurrent defensive reforms undertaken under the aegis of the Counter-Reformation by clergy who were as revulsed as the people at large by the many excesses at hand.

The tension continues to this day. Although the Roman Church has shed medieval excesses, the problem of individual freedom of religious thought and action is inevitably pitted against the authority of the church as institution. What suffers now, as then, are the selected common sacred traditions of Protestants and Catholics — innocent "victims" of both extremes. Those victims include the continuity of apostolic succession and all that that implies for the delivery of the sacraments and for true ecumenicity.

Would the Roman Church have reformed herself from within? Probably not.

Could reforms have been instituted from without and still preserved the essential traditions except for the papacy? Very likely, but speculation is an academic exercise.

Can residual traditions be maintained, or even restored where they are lacking? Undoubtedly, if the people desire to do so.

Why would the people not wish to do so? For all the reasons of distrust, ignorance, and the need for individual freedom that prompted and propelled the forces of the Reformation.

Is this good? Only ignorance is bad.

Is this ignorance of which we speak intellectual ignorance, lack of information? Partly. But it is also partly the failure to recognize the symbiotic relationship of the individual members to a valid and vital institution perpetuating Christ's corporate mystical presence on earth.

Lastly, some of this ignorance is based upon indifference. And that is the worst sort.

CHAPTER V

The Church of England

"The Church as it now stands no human power can save."

— *Thomas Arnold, 1795-1842*

"The Church of England is ripe for dissolution."

— *Jeremy Bentham, 1748-1832*

A. Catholic and Reformed

The schizoid nature of the Anglican Church can easily be discerned both by those within the church and by those looking at it from the outside. This observation constitutes a compliment and a criticism.

There are advantages and disadvantages to a two-sided church. Some see the church as comprehensive; others consider it wishy-washy, hopelessly unable to make up its mind as to its true nature. Many wonder how an institution that claims to have at least some of "the truth" can wear such mutually exclusive badges as evangelical and Anglo-Catholic, middle-of-the-road and liberal, autonomous and international. In its defense, the Anglican Church claims by its actions and pronouncements that, because of its catholicity, it can be all things to all people. It also claims that it is truly Catholic in the historic and doctrinal senses as well as truly reformed in keeping with the tenets of the Reformation. Its parallel characteristics are, therefore, respect for learning — gained through both its Catholic heritage and its Reformation refinement — and tolerance — a function of the

Reformation. Its three foundations for faith are scripture, tradition, and reason.

There is no doubt that the Anglican Church is the ancient Catholic Church of the British Isles. Since the arrival of Christianity with St. Patrick in Ireland in the 5th century, and its reintroduction by St. Augustine in Kent in 597, the Church of England has held to the ancient scriptures, creeds, sacraments, and apostolic ministry. Later, with the Norman Conquest, the church in England was brought into closer administrative and spiritual connection with the church in Rome. Admittedly, at the time of the Reformation there was a break with the pope; yet, according to Bishop Jewel of Salisbury, in his "Apology for the Church of England," the church "planted no new religion, but only renewed the old that was undoubtedly founded and used by the Apostles of Christ and other holy Fathers in the primitive Church." It did not occur to most, clergy or laity, that the internal reform undertaken involved more than a break with a foreign power.

But continuity alone is not sufficient to establish and maintain the Catholicity of a church. The test is this: Does the church hold the Catholic faith as imbedded in church tradition, honor the Bible, retain the threefold ministry of bishops, priests, and deacons, and provide the seven sacraments to its people?

The answer would seem to be affirmative. The Anglican Church subscribes to the three historic creeds: the Apostles', the Nicene, and the Athanasian. It does not doubt the authenticity of holy scripture. It ordains deacons and priests and consecrates bishops. It faithfully administers the sacraments of Baptism and the Eucharist and makes available the other five to those who wish them.

But this half of the nature of the Anglican Church must not eclipse the other half. Some people may regret the infusion of Protestantism, but none can deny its presence. Most will admit that the break with the papacy freed the church from undesirable foreign political control and eliminated many abuses stemming from the sale of indulgences, benefices, and dispensations. In addition, Christians in the British Isles now enjoyed a spiritual freedom to read and interpret the Bible, to pray, and to worship as never before.

The comprehensiveness of the Anglican Communion is not merely a function of its two halves, Catholicism and Protestantism, but entails an array of factions within each division. Over the last 450 or so years there have been Low Churchmen, Anglo-Catholics, Liberals, Evangelicals, and Broad Churchmen. Except perhaps to those on the ultra-Protestant end of the spectrum, the Anglican Church is a mish-mash with few redeeming features. What the "Catholic" side has overlooked in this regard is the tolerance fostered by such an arrangement. However, what the "Protestants" in the church have failed to recognize may be much more important: The glue that has held the church together is nothing more, nothing less than the Catholic faith.

B. King Henry VIII

In no discussion of the Church of England can Henry VIII be omitted. To Anglicans and Englishmen in general he is a source of embarrassment; to Roman Catholics he is the sure source of their rejection of Anglicanism as a schismatical and heretical branch of Christendom. History records Henry's life as one of egoism, hedonism, and murder. Under the guise of moral right or public policy he sought and achieved personal desires of every sort. He married six times, made others pay with their lives for his mistakes, and ruled England with an iron hand. The ironies are that England enjoyed a comparatively peaceful existence under him during a time of war and religious strife on the Continent and that Pope Leo X awarded him, in 1521, the title "Defender of the Faith" for a treatise he wrote against Martin Luther. Thoroughly dissolute in his personal life, Henry VIII was nevertheless thoroughly orthodox in his spiritual life.

In the popular conception Henry VIII "founded" the Church of England. As the story goes, because Henry wanted to divorce his wife, Katharine of Aragon, to marry Anne Boleyn, to which the pope would not give his consent, the King set up his own church.

Matters were actually much more complicated. Henry had originally received a papal dispensation to marry Katharine, his elder brother's widow, shortly after his accession to the throne in 1509. Katharine produced six children, but only one, Mary I, survived infancy. Henry was obsessed with the notion of having a male heir and sought to divorce Katharine on the grounds that the papal dispensation granted him had been illegal. Katharine resisted steadfastly, and Pope Clement VII, clearly under the influence of Katharine's nephew, Holy Roman Emperor Charles V, refused to invalidate Henry's marriage. He did authorize, however, a commission to decide the issue in England. However, because Katharine did not recognize the jurisdiction of the court, the matter was removed to Rome in 1529. Furious, Henry initiated a policy of anticlericalism that he fully expected would force the pope to accede to his demand. He insisted that all ecclesiastical legislation be subject to royal approval and stopped all payments of annates to Rome. The pope did not give in on the divorce issue, but he did permit the appointment of Henry's nominee as Archbishop of Canterbury, Thomas Cranmer, whereupon Cranmer immediately granted Henry his annulment and crowned Anne Boleyn, whom Henry had already secretly married, Queen of England. The pope excommunicated Henry. Henry, in turn, pushed through the Act of Supremacy in 1534, making him Supreme Governor of the Church of

England. If the Church of England was "founded" by Henry VIII, this was the year in which he did it.

If Pope Clement had also excommunicated all of England, or had invited all those loyal to him to withdraw, the story would have taken a different turn. But apparently he was not concerned that grace could not be found in this "new" church and did neither. If he had been, he would not have permitted his flock to continue to partake of invalid sacraments or he would have sent priests loyal to him to England to rescue the flock.

But let us be fair. Clement died in September 1534. Let us therefore assume he simply did not have time to carry out such plans.

Clement was succeeded by Paul III. Surely, a decision would be made by him, given the gravity of the situation. But no, all fifteen years of his reign went by, and Paul did absolutely nothing to help the people of England. King Henry died in 1547, leaving the pope two whole years in which to institute changes if he had deemed them necessary. One wonders whether Paul thought England needed help.

Pope Julius III followed Paul and reigned for six years. During this time he seemed not to be aware of the plight of the English people. Upon his death Marcellus II ascended the throne of Peter. But we certainly cannot fault this man, for he died just three weeks after his election.

From May 1555 to August 1559 Paul IV reigned as pope. Righteous, strong, even rigid, he did nothing during his four years to save his English spiritual flock from the "false" ministrations of the "new" English church. His successor, Pius IV, zealous and indefatigable reformer and archadversary of Protestantism, did nothing either during his six years as pontiff.

With St. Pius V, who took over in 1566, things would surely be different. He has been described as determined, downright stubborn, and excessively pious and could therefore be expected to correct the egregious neglect shown by his six predecessors. And, indeed, he did undertake negotiations with Queen Elizabeth in an attempt to recall English Christians to Roman loyalty. But Henry's daughter by Anne Boleyn was not to be convinced that there was any advantage to a link-up with Rome. Ten years passed, and English Christians still went their accustomed way, receiving all the sacraments from their church, and following the leadership of Henry's primate, Thomas Cranmer, they continued in full communion with Rome. As far as is known, no clergy protested against attendance at Anglican services, and none tried to ordain specifically Roman priests or to establish seminaries for a particularly Roman theological education.

Finally, in 1570, and thirty-six years after King Henry had ostensibly "founded" the Church of England, St. Pius V excommunicated Queen Elizabeth and all adherents of the Church of England. More than a generation had passed during which people had partaken of all the sacraments for their whole lives before a pope saw fit to punish them for membership in Henry's "creation."

What is one to make of this curious action? It must be seen for what it was—pure politics and nothing else. For, if Pius's six predecessors failed in their duty to excommunicate England, the infallible judgment of the papacy in matters of faith and morals cannot be taken seriously. If they acted correctly—whether for political or religious reasons—then Pius himself must be held accountable for gross misjudgment. The fact is the Reformation popes had no idea that Henry had "founded" another church. They were simply resisting political posturing by rebel countries and parties favorable to civil power as they had already a number of times in France, the German states, and Italy when papal control was questioned.

The Church of Rome has yet to explain its action.

C. Faith

Faith is, generally speaking, an unquestioning belief that does not require unequivocal evidence. It can, in fact, be an entire system of religious beliefs.

Every religious group, every church, insists upon adherence to some statement from its members, else there would be no coherence of belief. At its most basic, the Christian professes the belief that Jesus is the Son of God. Certainly, this is the *sine qua non* for Baptism.

Out of this fundamental belief developed, over the years, the historic creeds and confessions of the various churches. Of the three subscribed to by the Anglican Church the Apostles' Creed stands apart as the simplest, most direct, and most widespread within Christendom. It expresses belief in Christ as a member of the Trinity: God the Father, Jesus Christ His only Son, and the Holy Spirit. It adds a statement about the Communion of Saints and the forgiveness of sins. It is a forward-looking creed, with emphasis on life after death.

The Nicene Creed is a confession of faith originally adopted at the first Nicene Council in A.D. 325 and later expanded to forms accepted throughout most of Christianity. Its statement is largely theological, defining Jesus as "the only Son of God, eternally begotten of the Father, God from God, Light from Light, true God from true God, begotten, not made, of one Being with the Father." We received this creed from the East, but since the sixth century it has been the creed used at the Eucharist in the West as well. Of the three creeds the Nicene Creed is the one binding together Anglicans, Roman Catholics, and the Orthodox.

The Athanasian Creed, like the Nicene, is theological in thrust. It is more recent than the other two creeds and of unknown origin. It has never been accepted in the Eastern Church and is seldom used as part of worship services in the West. It was useful once in combatting the heresy of Arianism, but its function today is slight. Though almost technical or legal in language and scope, it is nevertheless a valuable document of faith.

Relegated to the back of the Prayer Book, like the Athanasian Creed, are the Thirty-nine Articles. This statement of doctrine, however, does not share the same universality of acceptance within Christianity or, for that matter, within the Anglican Communion. Only the clergy have been required to give vocal assent to its principles, although many of the laity have found the Articles in agreement with their beliefs. It was composed at a time when the church thought it imperative to pinpoint its disagreements with Rome and the Anabaptists. The list contained forty-two articles in the beginning, but by 1563 it had been reduced to thirty-nine. In some ways the Articles resemble the various "confessions" in use on the Continent; but they are less belligerent in their wording. Over the years, concessions to subscribing clergy have been made, and ordinands are now expected to give only their general consent and not to express absolute accord with every single article. Much has been made over the tone of the Articles, which, through interpretation or rationalization, can be shown to be dangerously anti-Catholic in places. Yet nobody takes them to be a definitive statement of faith.

The Book of Common Prayer is actually the center of the church's declaration of faith, for it contains not only the liturgy of the church but also the creeds, the pastoral offices, the ordinals, the psalter, the lectionary, the catechism, and the Articles. And, what is most important, everything in it is based on holy scripture, the ultimate test of all matters of faith. Article VI makes this abundantly clear: "Holy Scripture containeth all things necessary to salvation: so that whatsoever is not read therein, nor may be proved thereby, is not to be required of any man, that it should be believed as an article of the Faith, or be thought requisite or necessary to salvation. In the name of the Holy Scripture we do understand those canonical Books of the Old and New Testament, of whose authority was never any doubt in the Church." And then are listed the names and number of the canonical books.

But one thing must be kept in mind. The Church is the mother of the Bible in the sense that she collected and approved the individual books. This places tradition on a par with scripture to the extent that only the Church has the duty and the right to the interpretation of scripture. In a canon of 1571 all clergy are enjoined "never to teach anything in a sermon which is to be religiously held and believed by the people except what is agreeable to the doctrine of the Old and New Testaments and what the Catholic Fathers and ancient bishops have collected from the same doctrine." Such a statement logically rules out both the infallibility of scripture and of a single bishop, the pope.

Ideally, then, interpretation should be carried out, as "the mind of the Church," through councils. Of course, this process would not eliminate disagreement, for there can be honest differences of opinion as to the meaning of scripture or tradition. Neither would a conciliar decision be cast in concrete for all time if it could be shown that a mistake had been made. In its decennial assemblies Lambeth could function as a council for the entire Anglican Communion. It is doubtful that harm would come to the individual national churches; in fact, the people, laity and clergy alike, would repose greater trust in their church, knowing that its "mind" had spoken on issues of great import. The present controversy over ordaining women is one case in point. What are the people at large to think when the American church takes it upon itself to forge forward on an issue that clearly places it at odds not only with other communions but also with segments of its own? There is no unity of faith in such action.

D. Worship

Just as unity in faith is desirable for many reasons, so is a fundamental unity in worship. That unity must transcend time and the idiosyncrasies of the worship leader. That unity must be expressed in service books handed down, revised in keeping with doctrine, over the centuries.

At the time of its composition during Reformation days the Book of Common Prayer took the place of the breviary, the missal, the manual, the pontifical, and the processional. Archbishop Cranmer's intention had obviously been to provide an order of service which would be followed throughout all the churches of the realm. Queen Elizabeth confirmed this intention by the Act of Uniformity, which carried with it stiff penalties for any who dared eliminate or substitute prayers for those authorized. It was hoped that such a prayer book would draw together all believers. It did not. The Papalists went one way, and the Puritans the other way. For the former, the new liturgy was possibly heretical; for the latter, it smacked of Romanism. But the book did establish an order within the Church of England that persisted for almost two centuries.

However, with religious revivals of both Catholic and evangelical emphasis in force throughout the 18th and 19th centuries, it was soon discovered that the services officially provided were not sufficient to enhance the new spiritual life. Thus, additions, accretions, subtractions, dislocations developed in order to satisfy the perceived need. To be sure, the Prayer Book was the *standard* for virtually all parishes, yet it was difficult to find a parish in which some departure from the standard was not evident. Sometimes the changes were trivial;

sometimes they were of a more serious order, such as the omission of one of the creeds or even alterations within the Canon of the Eucharist itself. As an act of near desperation, the judicial committee of the Privy Council wrote in 1868: "It is not open to a Minister of the Church, or even to their Lordships in advising Her Majesty as the highest Ecclesiastical Tribunal of Appeal, to draw a distinction, in acts which are a departure from or violation of the Rubric, between those which are important and those which are trivial."

Less than a hundred years later, serious tampering with the liturgy began after World War II, in 1947, with the establishment of the Church of South India, a curious conglomerate of Anglican and non-Anglican churches in need of a liturgy that would serve all elements. All the member churches wanted the new united church to have a liturgy. Those who came from a liturgical background, particularly the Anglicans, wanted to retain a familiar feature of their church. Those from non-liturgical backgrounds felt they had been missing something. Out of fear of appearing to dominate, the Anglicans could not impose their Prayer Book upon the new united body. The consensus was, therefore, that the Church of South India should write its own liturgy. The model was based upon Dom Gregory Dix's suggestion in his *Shape of the Liturgy* that recourse be to the liturgies of the early church, not to present-day prayer books. The Church of South India was much more successful in its endeavors than anyone had expected, and the liturgy of the "Lord's Supper" that it produced in 1950 subsequently became an entire prayer book called the Book of Common Worship.

No doubt, the Church of South India scholars intended to create a worship pattern that could be used in the developing united churches throughout the world. It did not turn out that way, though, for the predicted hodge-podge union schemes did not come off to any great extent. Instead, new, or revised, liturgies — some of them following the model of the CSI liturgy—gained considerable publicity, and the rollercoaster effect took over, leading first to *Prayer Book Studies* in this country and *Prayer Book Revision in the Church of England* (SPCK), and ultimately to our present 1979 Book of Common Prayer.

If it were not for what many consider to be substantial doctrinal changes due to the revision of the 1928 Prayer Book—some of which changes were discussed earlier—most members of the Episcopal Church would probably admit that periodic revision is healthy. Most revisions seek to retain the flavor or tone of the prior prayer book while also emphasizing clarity of presentation. The latter may entail updating the language. There may also be an attempt to make the new book more comprehensive and thus more applicable to diverse demands within the church. The comprehensive nature of the book may dictate the inclusion of more rubrics and allow for enrichment of ceremonial.

To a great extent, all this has been accomplished in the 1979 Book of Common Prayer. Even a certain synchronic unity in worship has been achieved and extended by a growing preference for the Eucharist at the principal service on Sunday as well as at an earlier hour; by a choice between Rite I and Rite II, where the former preserves much from the 1928; by a similarity with the Roman Catholic Mass (which was, because of a lack of tradition in the use of the vernacular, based on much gleaned from Anglican services); and by the tendency in the Protestant churches to ape (or actually use parts of) the Book of Common Prayer. What disturbs people in their worship is the lack of unity with the *past*, a loss of the penitential flavor of the old book, and a forced congruity with the present, reflected largely in the colloquial language. These people cannot understand why the 1928 Book is not permitted alongside the 1979 since the former satisfies the missing element of diachronic unity, preserves a legitimate tone of repentance in a shameless age, and still closely resembles other extant, non-revised Anglican liturgies. Similar complaints can be found among Roman Catholics who miss the Tridentine Mass.

Why are the objectors ignored? If one may theorize, the reasoning probably goes something like this. There is virtue in unity—and we have already said as much—and the unity applies just as much to the unity of each major segment of the church—that is, to each national expression of the whole—as it does to the entire Anglican (or Roman) Communion. Secondly, there has been an obvious trend throughout many of the mainline Western churches, Protestant and Catholic alike, to employ similar forms of liturgy and ceremonial. In short, we are growing closer together, and this is a good thing. Lastly, if the Christian religion and its worship experience are for all people at all times, it must have the appearance of relevancy to the present.

There are some things right about this theory and some things wrong. First of all, Christians agree that Christ's message is applicable to all people and at all times. Second, only a blind person would deny that there has been a leveling trend at work among the churches: added ceremonial where there was little or none, reduction in formality when form seemed to get in the way of substance, the infusion of spontaneity in worship, prayers for cooperation among churches for the public social good, prayers for the environment, more prayers for special occasions, and so on. But all of these ostensibly laudable features are pragmatically predicated on the assumption that the present has greater stability than the past, that relevance counts for more than tradition, and that the future will resemble the present.

It has always been assumed that part of the genius of the Anglican Communion has been the lack of strict uniformity of worship that has permitted services conducted with the utmost simplicity as well as services with elaborate ceremonial. The supporters of the 1928 Book of Common Prayer argue that the authorization of its continued use would be merely another facet of the Church's benevolent permissiveness. Might the proponents of the 1979 Book join forces with the supporters of the 1928 in an ever so slightly doctored version of Edward Gibbon's statement in Chapter 2 of his *Decline and Fall of the Roman Empire* and assert: "The various modes of worship which prevailed in the Roman world were all considered by the people as equally true; by the philosopher [or theologian], as equally false; and by the magistrate [or hierarchy], as equally useful. And thus toleration produced not only mutual indulgence, but even religious concord"?

CHAPTER VI

The Anglican Church in the United States

"When I mention religion, I mean the Christian religion; and not only the Christian religion, but the Protestant religion; and not only the Protestant religion but the Church of England."

— *Henry Fielding, 1707-1754*

"Mother Church."

— *Tertullian, c.160-c.225, Ad Martyras*

A. Beginnings

Every schoolchild knows that the first permanent English settlement in the New World was at Jamestown in Virginia in 1607. The English had tried to establish colonies in America several decades before that, but each attempt ended in tragedy. The best-known of the ill-fated settlements was that of the "lost colony" established by Sir Walter Raleigh on Roanoke Island, Virginia. Raleigh's half-brother, Sir Humphrey Gilbert, also tried and failed in Newfoundland. The two of them made another attempt on the island of Monhegan, Maine, in the spring of 1607. Present on each expedition were clergymen of the Church of England who had made the hazardous journey not for the purpose of establishing the Church in America but to minister to the settlement group. The clergymen's presence signaled little more than the Englishman's perpetual desire to be surrounded by familiar things: High tea in the desert, Sunday services in the outback of a new land.

The real reason for England's colonization of the New World was economic, not religious. The country was facing the prospect of a severe depression if it did not discover new raw materials that it could use in such industries as shipbuilding, smelting, and woolen manufacture. It hoped especially that the New World would provide lumber from its many reported virgin forests. There were, of course, other reasons for planning expeditions, among them the desire to check the ever-growing power of Spain; but mainly, England desperately needed to bolster its economy through settlements in America that would regularly return much-needed raw materials.

Thus, the efforts to give permanence to the New World excursions continued. In 1606 King James I granted a charter to the London Company, whose task was to transport a group to an area in the territory of Virginia where they would search for mineral deposits, begin farming and some simple manufacturing, and look for a northwest passage to the Orient. We know from the records that an Anglican priest by the name of Robert Hunt was among those one hundred colonists who appeared one spring day in 1607 on the bank of the James River at what was to be Jamestown. Captain John Smith tells us about the makeshift church in the woods — a board for a table between two trees, a sail for cover, some logs and stumps to sit on — and the daily Morning and Evening Prayer, the two sermons on Sunday, and the quarterly Communion service. It is amazing that so much spiritual nourishment was provided; but we have to wonder whether it would have been so readily consumed if the law had not required compliance on pain of harsh punishment.

In 1624 the colony became a royal province, and remained one until the Revolution. The royal governors vigorously promoted the official religion. Clergy had to swear that they were properly ordained and would conform to the Church of England in every way. The clergy received their salary through mandatory tithes collected from the people. One can imagine how little toleration there was for non-conformists and Roman Catholics.

In 1687 King James II, a Roman Catholic, issued an edict intended to secure religious liberty for all, but particularly for Roman Catholics in the colonies. But its effects were short-lived because William and Mary came to the throne one year later and reinstated all the former restrictions on Roman Catholics while granting to Protestant dissenters many more liberties.

From the beginning till the end of the 17th century parish size was a problem. Jamestown, the only town in the area, was extremely small. Most people lived and worked on plantations and farms strung along the north and south banks of the James River. This meant that the confines of a parish could be so extensive as to inhibit all but the most infrequent contact with persons from contiguous areas, including clergy. It was an awkward situation, for the parish was a unit incorporating not only the church, but also the courts. As more people came to the colony, the parishes were reduced somewhat in size, but they were still too large to be adequately served by one clergyman. Imagine having to travel twenty or more miles on a pig path to a chapel or a private home to conduct services on a Sunday in all kinds of weather! And then imagine how you would feel if nobody, or only a handful, showed up for worship since they too had to face all the hardships!

Obviously, laymen had to take over many of the liturgical duties of the clergy. Most were not authorized to write their own sermons, but had to rely on printed ones. Of course, they could not administer the sacraments. Under such difficult circumstances, it is hardly surprising that a certain laxness set in. Few of the principal feast days were celebrated; the sacraments were often improperly administered. The fact that, despite concerns among the church hierarchy in England, the colonists treated these deficiencies lightly gives us a clue to the genesis of general disregard for order and ceremonial so typical of Americans. There were even instances where parishes, in their zeal to attract anyone of good moral character to serve a church, appointed clergy without episcopal ordination to officiate in Anglican parishes.

And the situation became much worse before it became better. By the end of the 17th century most of the parishes had no clerical leadership, and those that did suffered from the direction of men of inadequate training and questionable character. Membership declined catastrophically, so that at one point hardly five percent of the people belonged. The colonies desperately needed their own bishop instead of having to rely on the jurisdiction of the far distant Bishop of London. Luckily, an intermediate step was taken by a farsighted Bishop of London, Henry Compton, who, in 1689, appointed James Blair the first commissary to Virginia, a position incorporating important non-sacramental, administrative functions. Blair was a man well-suited to the task. He gained the full support of the Crown and raised clerical salaries, increased the authority of vestries, and saw to it that the clergy were represented at governmental level. He also urged and engineered the education of clergy, many of whom, completely unlettered, had become indolent, indifferent, immoral, and drunken, by finagling a charter for the College of William and Mary, the second institution of higher learning in America. He was elected its first president, but soon became disheartened when so few enrolled. Reliance on clergy educated and ordained in England continued, and in his recruitment Blair was notably successful. By the time of his death Blair had managed to fill most of the vacant parishes in Virginia.

There was much scene-shifting at this time, from Virginia to Maryland to the Carolinas and Georgia.

Where royal provinces were established, the Anglican Church eventually thrived. The Church was slow to move north, and it was not until 1695 that Christ Church in Philadelphia, the first Anglican parish in Pennsylvania, was established. Two years later Trinity Church was founded in New York. Churches in Delaware began appearing not long thereafter.

New England was the last area to be invaded by Anglicans — and that is exactly how the Puritans saw their coming. When Robert Ratcliffe, an Anglican priest from England, arrived in the Massachusetts Bay Colony in 1686, he was not happily received. For a good quarter of a century England had been upset with the Puritans' political and ecclesiastical disobedience. Charles II was in no mood to put up with resistance to Ratcliffe's founding there an Anglican parish. He reminded the Puritans how much *they* had chafed at persecution and urged them to be tolerant and understanding of Anglicans. His pleadings were to no avail. In retaliation, the King had the Massachusetts charter legally revoked. But even with a royal government in operation in Massachusetts, the stubborn Puritans refused to cooperate. Disruption followed in 1688 when the Stuart dynasty ran into difficulties, and the Puritans were hopeful of regaining their charter. Increase Mather, a fiery old codger, succeeded in getting the charter back, but only at the expense of a clause which eliminated any test of religion in order for one to vote or hold office.

The history of Anglicanism in the rest of New England proceeded from Rhode Island in 1700 to Connecticut in 1706, where considerable strength was developed first in Stratford and then in Fairfield. In New Hampshire a parish at Plymouth, then known as Strawberry Bank, was established as early as 1640, but did not really succeed until 1734. Maine followed with one parish in 1761, but the Puritans continued to offer virulent resistance throughout New England, probably as much because the

Church had the support of the Crown as for religious reasons. It became increasingly obvious that the only hope for true success lay in securing the episcopate on this side of the Atlantic, a hope not to be realized until America broke loose politically from England.

B. The Eighteenth Century

The story of the church in the 17th century does not end as abruptly as indicated, for there is a great deal that could be said about the Puritans, the Separatists, the Quakers and the Baptists in New England, the Roman Catholics in Maryland, and others. But, as far as the Church of England in America goes, the truly important story of the 18th century is that of the acquisition of the episcopate.

In the years immediately following the Revolution the church was in a lamentable state. There was once again a shortage of clergy; there was demoralization in the ranks of the non-Loyalists; there were defections to other denominations; there was no center of authority; there was no canonical way of perpetuating the church.

Fortunately, three remarkable men appeared on the scene, two from the mid-Atlantic area and one from New England. The spread could only have been better had there also been someone from the South.

William Smith (1727-1803) was a priest from Maryland serving Chester Parish in 1780 when he decided to invite three clergymen and a dozen laymen to discuss and evaluate the condition of the Anglican Church. They essentially constituted themselves the "Protestant Episcopal Church in Maryland" and demanded of the state certain fundamental legal rights, including ownership of property formerly held by the established church. A formal declaration to this effect was made at a second assembly in 1783. The assembly then proceeded to elect Smith the first bishop of Maryland. For lack of consecrators Smith remained a mere priest, but he had had a tremendous effect on church-state relations.

At the same time in New England efforts were afoot to secure the episcopate for the new country. In March 1783, ten priests got together secretly and recommended sending either Jeremiah Leaming or Samuel Seabury to England for consecration. Leaming acknowledged the honor, but begged off because of his age. Seabury accepted readily and set sail for London, arriving there in July. There he discovered the English bishops would consecrate him only upon two conditions, namely, that he show unequivocally that Connecticut was in favor of his election and subsequent elevation and that he swear his allegiance to the Crown. He was prepared to prove that Connecticut desired his consecration, but his conscience would not allow him to serve as an American bishop whose episcopal loyalty was to England. He therefore refused their offer and traveled to Scotland where he was duly consecrated in the cathedral at Aberdeen on November 14, 1784. He returned to Connecticut in June 1785 and immediately ordained four men to the diaconate.

While Seabury was away in England and Scotland, another event was taking place in America. An informal meeting of clergy and laymen took place in New Brunswick, New Jersey, in May 1784. The meeting was the result of an impetus provided by an extraordinary man named William White (1748-1836), rector of Christ Church, Philadelphia. Although basically distrustful of bishops, White nevertheless believed in the apostolic succession and was at the point of despair that the United States would ever receive the episcopate. He therefore proposed, first anonymously in an article and then at the meeting, that a convention be called at which lay and clerical delegates in equal numbers be empowered to make several crucial decisions. Among them would be the decision to administer their own ordination.

That convention was held several days later in Philadelphia. The group stated its determination to regulate its own affairs free from control by England and affirmed its belief in the threefold ministry and the historic liturgy of the Church of England. In October 1784 a similar convention met in New York and adopted a set of virtually identical resolutions. The members recommended that state conventions elect bishops to be seated at a General Convention to be held in Philadelphia in September 1785. William White was elected bishop of Pennsylvania, and Samuel Provoost and David Griffith were chosen from New York and Virginia, respectively.

Seven states sent representatives to the General Convention. New England did not participate, perhaps because they felt Bishop Seabury would not be well received.

The Convention succeeded in framing a constitution and establishing the procedure for securing the consecration of White, Provoost, and Griffith. Once permission had been secured from England, White and Provoost departed for London. Griffith had in the meantime taken ill and could not go along. On February 4, 1787 White and Provoost were consecrated in Lambeth Chapel and returned immediately to America. The country now had the requisite number of three bishops for the consecrating of others. Its separate life had begun.

C. The Oxford Movement

The very nature of the modern Anglican Communion as a living spectrum of High and Low churchmanship had its public origin in the year 1833 when several Anglican clergymen at Oriel College, Oxford University, undertook, under the aegis of the Oxford Movement, to revive what they saw as a bland expression of Christianity. In July of that year a priest named John Keble preached a powerful sermon critical of the Church's overwhelming

Protestant stance, which he dubbed "On the National Apostasy." Several days later a meeting was held at Hadleigh, Suffolk, in the rectory of Hugh James Rose, the so-called "Cambridge originator of the Oxford movement," at which it was resolved that all would uphold "the apostolic succession and the integrity of the Prayer Book."

Inspired by the prospect of reintroducing certain Roman Catholic doctrines and ritualistic practices, John Henry Newman, another of the clergymen, began to popularize the movement by writing and distributing tracts in a series called *Tracts for the Times*. Shortly thereafter, Keble and a third cleric, Edward Bouverie Pusey, joined him in the effort. They became known as the Tractarians. They considered the Anglican Church "a true branch or portion of the one Holy, Catholic and Apostolic Church of Christ." In fact, for them it held the largest part of the truth. They taught that the Evangelicals and Non-Conformists held only a small part of the truth and that Rome held an "excess" of truth. These facts, as the Tractarians saw them, made of the Church of England a *via media* between Rome and the Evangelicals. Thus was the "bridge" nature of the Anglican Church defined and promoted.

The Oxford Movement emphasized the need to offer God the most complete and beautiful worship possible. For example, the church buildings themselves should be pleasing in every way; the services should be full of hymn singing and the intoning of the liturgy; colorful vestments should be in evidence. Although there was to be first an appeal to the senses, in no way was the scriptural and traditional nature of church doctrine to be neglected. It was an ideal joining of substance and effect, and this ideal has persisted to this day in Anglo-Catholic parishes throughout the Communion.

In an effort to deepen devotion to the Bible, Keble, Newman, and especially Pusey established a number of sisterhoods, the first in 1845, and a lesser number of brotherhoods. These religious communities focused much of their activity on social work. The responsibility of Christians to their society has, contrary to the perceptions of many of Low-church bent, been a persistent theme of Anglo-Catholicism, a "ritualistic" expression into which the Oxford Movement evolved after the death of its founders. To a large degree, this commitment, which recognizes various minorities, explains why today's homosexuals gravitate to Anglo-Catholic parishes. The Oxford Movement and its continuing effects therefore point up another trait of the Anglican Church: it reaches deep within and grasps aggressively outward as well. Again, the adhesive is Catholicism.

But not everyone saw the logic or desirability of the Movement, and resistance to it even reached the point of rioting at times. We are past that point today, but the tension between the Protestant and Catholic aspects of the Church still obtains. As long as that tension represents no more than a dynamic, moving the Church forward to greater truth, it is good. When one side overwhelms the other, or causes defections—John Henry Newman and Henry Edward Manning left Anglicanism for Romanism—it is bad. And this is the danger we face today, for there are many who see the Anglican Church inundated by new waves of the gnostic and secular humanist elements of Protestantism and who, in desperation, seek spiritual serenity elsewhere. Saddest of all, though, is the growth of a group today who characterize themselves as traditionalists, whose spiritual home was, and must always be, that "best truth," the Anglican truth of which the Tractarians spoke and wrote, and who have been cast into the limbo of disregard.

D. Clergy

For many the very words "clergy," "priest," "bishop," "minister," "Father" (now "Mother" too?) conjure up emotions based on fear, suspicion, and distrust, but for others, of course, also comfort, trust, and love. The spectrum runs from the pathologically anti-clerical to the fanatically religious. Most of us fit well within those extremes, but some cannot shake the notion that the authority the clergy represent poses a threat as well as an assurance. The reaction is not all that different from the way many feel about members of the other learned professions: about their professors, their lawyers, and their physicians, all of whom to a greater or lesser extent hold in their power the advancement, the defense or prosecution, or the health of their clients.

Ideally, of course, there should be a love, not a love/hate relationship between the people and their clergy, for it is the clergy's professional business to display and teach love and understanding. Their explanation — or excuse — for falling short of the ideal is that they are, after all, only human.

That argument did not use to work with the people, for, although they comprehended rationally that clergy are indeed people like themselves, they were just as aware that clergy are also people set apart by ordination, an act very different from, say, a licensing procedure to authorize the practice of law or medicine. It was felt the cleric's power is not so dependent upon his or her knowledge or skill as it is upon that Power from beyond.

Before we consider why, in contrast to earlier times, the argument works very well today, let us see what the basis for the former position was.

The ladder of ordination is a three-rung affair for most Christians, even shorter for many Protestant denominations who lack one or two of the rungs. Those steps, in ascending order, are for the making of deacons, the ordaining of priests, and the consecrating of bishops. In actuality, for most clerical members of the Catholic churches the ladder has only two rungs, that of deacon and that of priest, for very few become bishops. The center rung, that of the priesthood, is the key, for it represents the completion of the step taken in the diaconate, and it is essential to the third step, that of becoming a bishop.

It is not our place here to debate the technical differences among the three ranks of clergy, nor is it our intention to subject to scrutiny the many ordinals in use over the centuries, Anglican and other, in an effort to establish what others, far more competent, have been unable to do: namely, to determine the proper form, matter, intention, and instruments of the process. Not only do the people as a whole not know anything profound about all this; they do not care what is done as long as they have the assurance that *something* has set their clergy apart. This is not to denigrate the people, nor is it to suggest that they could not understand, with motivation and learning, anything that a cleric could comprehend. It simply does not matter to them in the way it *ought to* matter to the clergy. The people depend on the clergy to *know* certain things; the clergy count on the people *not* to know those same things. Out of this relationship has grown up a two-way trust.

There are those who are convinced this trust has been broken.

First of all, however impressionistic the evidence may have been that the church's role in COCU was, and continues to be, improper, the parochial clergy and the hierarchy have done little to dispel the feeling among many that the church has sold its birthright by participating in an organization that will absorb the Episcopal

Church and thereby nullify its claim on the apostolic succession.

Secondly, although steps were taken through the use of trial liturgies and parish discussions of the proposed 1979 Prayer Book, many thousands of Episcopalians are still hard put to understand why, with all the other diversity in worship permitted in the church today, they may not continue to use the 1928 Prayer Book with the permission of the Presiding Bishop and individual diocesans. They argue cogently that, if the 1928 was theologically inoffensive before 1979, serious defects did not suddenly appear in 1979.

Thirdly, these same people cannot understand how a single diocese in the Anglican Communion, the Diocese of Massachusetts, was able to effect a momentous, worldwide change in the nature of the Church by electing and illegally consecrating a bishop unqualified for the position by assumed modern standards of education and pastoral experience, thereby jeopardizing ecumenical relations with the largest sister Catholic bodies in the world.

The answer, they reason, lies with the majority of priests and bishops who did not have, or dared not display, the knowledge and conviction requisite to their position as clergy and guides for their people. And this, they claim, is not in keeping with a church that has always prided itself on sound learning and the sharing of it in a democratic spirit. It may be instructive to note that in the new Prayer Book, pp.517-518, the following question of the bishop-elect, taken from the Examination portion of the ordinal for the Consecrating of Bishops, page 555 in the 1928 Book of Common Prayer, is strangely missing: *Bishop.* "Are you ready, with all faithful diligence, to banish and drive away from the Church all erroneous and strange doctrine contrary to God's Word; and both privately and openly to call upon and encourage others to the same?"

It may now be asked how it is that the humanity of the clergy is working to their advantage. It would seem, in fact, that their failure a) to withdraw from COCU in order to secure the apostolic succession; b) to urge the parallel use of the 1928 Prayer Book; and c) to resist the election of anybody as bishop not eminently qualified by Constitutional law and education would operate to their disadvantage.

The answer lies in the trend of the times. From the late 1960s on, a spirit of social and professional leveling has been in vogue in the United States. A generation unwilling to make judgments on any element of society left of center gave its approval to church union schemes while at the same time withholding its membership support year after year from mainline churches. In the Episcopal Church, communicant strength dwindled from 2,341,861 in 1968 to 1,963,625 in 1985, a loss of 378,236 members in a scant 17 years, as reported in the *1989 Episcopal Church Annual.* During the same period, baptized membership dropped from 3,588,435 to 2,972,607, a loss of 615,828 persons.[19] Instead of being seen as a cause for alarm, these losses prompted the clergy to take even more liberalizing steps in the hope of recapturing membership. One of the concurrent steps to enlarge the appeal of the church both within and without was the authorization of women priests. During the same period of membership drop, the number of clergy increased from 11,362 in 1968 to 14,482 in 1985, a gain of 3,120 or an increase of 28 percent.[20] The number of female clergy had gone from zero in 1975 to 796 in 1986, representing 28% of the total, as reported in a 1986 table contained in the 1989 *Yearbook of American and Canadian Churches*[21] Female seminarians in the Episcopal Church now constitute 38 percent of the total.

Nevertheless, the membership loss continues year after year, and the liberalizing of the church continues apace. One would think the hierarchy and parochial clergy would be in for big criticism. But no, except for a few strident, yet weak voices, accolades have generally followed. The Episcopal Church, and other denominations as well, have been congratulated on their general appeal, the relaxation of rules regarding the taking of communion, clergy appointments, pulpit exchange, the place of canon law, and ecumenical approaches.

It is certain that examples of questionable clerical conduct abound within every denomination, but it is always with a sense of despair that one observes mischief that is ignored and misbehavior that goes unpunished. Some of the mischief can reach the heights of accusation of heresy, but no follow-through is, in fairness to both sides, ever carried out. The misbehavior can, and usually does, involve some sexual aspect, but it can also be garden-variety crime. Let's look at some examples.

• "How did he bring the matter up? What were you doing when he told you he wanted a divorce?" I asked. "It was lunchtime," she said, "and he was sitting at the kitchen table eating a peanut butter and jelly sandwich. He simply said he wanted a divorce. Oh, and then he said he ought to get a drama prize for his acting over the last ten years."

Thus ended twenty-five years of marriage and began years of emotional chaos for a wife and four children. This man has now been married three times, totally disrupted two churches, and his bishop has yet to dismiss him. "Too many such problems," moaned the bishop. "I've got fifty similar cases on my desk at the moment." When the wayward minister appeared before his bishop after the second messy divorce and was asked to consider resignation, his lawyer son threatened legal action against the church, arguing that his father had invested too many years in the ministry to leave without a steady livelihood. The bishop gave his minister another church.

• Eugene Peterson, pastor of Christ Our King Presbyterian Church in Bel Air, Maryland, agreed in an article entitled "How Pure Must a Pastor Be?" "It's harder to detect integrity in pastors and Christian leaders than in anybody else. We're better at cover-up. We were brought up being con artists, and we improve at it as we get older."[22]

• "I have on good authority that Miss S--- is going to leave her house to the church," reported the vestryman. "After all, she never married and has only an estranged brother and a niece. Besides, the people of the church have been exceptionally good to her. In the last two years they have transported her everywhere and have even brought her most of her meals to the house."

Some years later Miss S--- left the house and all its furnishings — 99.9% of her estate — to a young divorced curate who had lavished attention on her. He received the $120,000 shortly after being indicted for embezzling another church of $66,000, which was repaid by a woman in another parish.

• "Is there another woman?" I asked. "No," answered my old friend and rector. "I'll ask you again," I said, "just as I did my college roommate." "No," answered the friend once again, just as had my roommate, also a clergyman.

Both were lying. The former dumped his wife for his director of Christian education; the latter his for a choir member in his church. In a recent unpublished paper, the Rt. Rev. David E. Richards states somewhat sympathetically: "The dilemma in many clergy marriages is how ... both the needs of the marriage and family [can] be met along with the demands of ministry." The bishop further states that the added burden of unpaid seminary tuition and expenses, coupled with typical day-to-day financial problems after appointment, contributes significantly to the increasing divorce rate among clergy. However, without realizing it, the bishop puts his finger on the root problem when he notes that more and more people are abandoning first careers and going to seminary and that "we are curiously [*sic*!] in a situation in which increasing numbers of persons seem to be willing to face such a circumstance."

The reasons they are willing to do so are, of course, complex; yet it is not unreasonable to suggest that the desire for power over people, driven by substantial egos, and the recognition that ultimately the ministry pays rather well in salary, benefits, and free or broken time play major parts in reaching a positive decision.

- "I don't know what she does upstairs in her office all the time. I think she's downright lazy," said the rector of his female assistant at 10 o'clock one morning as he reached for his new golf clubs in his office closet.

- "Did you see that hair?" inquired the rector of me. He was referring to his good-looking young female curate who had let down her long hair. "She's just trying to attract the men," he grumbled.

- "But what you have done is contrary to canon law, Father. See, it is written right here." "Bull shit, canon law is to be used for or against you, as circumstances dictate," replied the priest cynically.

- "I don't have to believe what I preach," said the minister. "Who can recognize insincerity, anyhow?"

- "I just want to be accepted as a 'real person' — like everybody else," whined the clergyman. His drinking and womanizing became legendary upon his departure.

- "Don't collect any more purses for him; he already thinks he's God," volunteered a clergyman's wife.

- "Do you mean your rabbi has not so much as telephoned, let alone come out?" "That's right," said the widow after a week's wait in vain. The Christian frowned and made a quick, and depressing, comparison with her own clergyman.

• "Old Mrs. K--- could use a visit," said the church secretary to the interim pastor. "She's a long-time member and is in X Nursing Home with a broken hip and pelvis." "She wouldn't know me," objected the priest, and went about his business. Later in the morning, the secretary made the same request of the new female assistant. "Oh, she's in D---. That's quite a place. She's being well cared for; she doesn't need me." Truer words were never spoken.

• A loyal, well-heeled parishioner wanted to discuss the many changes in his church at the local and national level and asked three of the clergy — all friends — to help him understand the church's ultraliberal position. "I don't want to talk about it," said all three. The man walked away from the church. Two years later, and still not a sign of concern by the clergy — not a visit, not a note, not even a phone call. His wife wrote the bishop a long letter describing her own heartsickness and asking for his help as chief pastor. He wrote, but avoided the hard questions.

The anecdotes are true, and they could go on. They are just a few random samples gathered over the last decade. Other, splashier, examples are easy to find on the national scene among the televangelists of late. Clergy of all ranks and all denominations are suffering from a loss of image among their people. The laity ask why *their* concerns, based as they often are upon physical and mental health needs, fundamental theological premises or simple, canonical expediencies, are less allowable among the clergy than the clergy's own frequent shirking of duty, timidity in the face of moral and ethical challenge, and personal immorality. It is fair to ask what it means to live and operate within the bounds of constituted authority, and to what extent one may be a noncon-formist.

As to the matter of divorce, Bishop Alexander D. Stewart, Executive Vice President of the (Episcopal) Church Pension Fund, reported privately to me that the Fund "cannot give any actual statistics because[,] frankly[,] we may have clergy who are divorced of whom we are totally unaware. Sometimes we even learn of the divorce and re-marriage when the man is applying for a retirement pension and we discover that the wife's name does not match the name that we have on his card." The bishop goes on to say that it might surprise me to know "that it is an incredibly small percentage that even assigns a portion of their eventual pension to their wife, or spouse." The problem of divorce among the clergy, though only one impediment to the creation of a proper example to their parishioners, is fast becoming a major area of sociological and statistical investigation. One work, *Episcopal Clergy Families in the 80's (April 1988)*, funded by grants from the Church Pension Fund, the Trinity Grants Board, and the Episcopal Church Founda-tion, examines in detail how the events in a clergyman's private life "may well influence the way he/she functions in various aspects of the ministry."

There are, to be sure, rotten apples in every profes-sion, but the ministry is different, and should tolerate far less bad fruit, because it is based on precept and example and on the assumption of the possession of some "mysti-cal" power by its practitioners. This concept is in opposi-tion to that of the other learned professions where results count for more than "profession." Medicine relies on the power of science; lawyering on the interpretation and implementation of the law; teaching on the education of individuals who must then demonstrate their compe-tence. Ideally, the ministry ought to incorporate all these features, for it must defend or combat science, rely on canon law and the tradition of the church, and be based on the ability to persuade. Unlike his outlook in the other professions, an individual cleric's attitude can immediately affect large numbers of people.

Until the third century and the Emperor Constantine there was no separate clerical class, although the notion of clergy probably originated as a combination of Greek and Jewish ideas. Upon his conversion to Christianity Constantine was quick to endow the Christian clergy with all the privileges previously enjoyed by the pagan priests and vestal virgins, which included exemption from certain taxes and public duties, allowing them an elite status that they have maintained in most denominations until this day. Originally, in the Gentile Church, the clergy exercised solely spiritual functions and were not, as today, concerned with managing an organization, raising money, or exercising some legislative effort. Most people recognize the value of an efficiently run organization, and no one belittles the honest efforts of clergy to raise money or to lobby for the general welfare, but more and more people are questioning the spiritual commitment of their clergy.

Anti-clericalism is not being advocated. The traditionalist advocates the reinstatement of the image of clergy as the prime example of the Christian life for the people under their charge. Mark B. Thompson, in his article, "Who Should Be Ordained?" accuses the clergy of frequent "incompetence" and says, "Notwithstanding the fact that we have many priests who simply carry their ordination around in their hip pocket, ordination to the priesthood should be considered primarily in the context of being the president of the local congregation, in all of its ramifications."[23] Those "ramifications" include the willingness to teach all sides of important church questions, the exhibiting of understanding and compassion in time of bereavement, and the meeting of needs occasioned by physical and psychic illness. It is a lot, but it is not too much to expect clergy to present to their flock, and to society at large, an image of uprightness in all matters, for otherwise it is inevitable they will be tarred with failure to practice what they are constrained to preach.

But such attitudes are not restricted to other denominations or to middle-of-the-road Episcopal parishes. Your writer remembers returning on Palm Sunday, 1988, to an Anglo-Catholic parish of which he and his family had been members some thirty years prior. Things had really changed. The story is worth telling.

On this Sunday the choir warmed up in their stalls for about twenty minutes prior to the start of the Solemn Eucharist, Rite I. The variety of casual clothing exhibited led your writer and his wife to look forward to the choir's vested reappearance.

After the Liturgy of the Palms, the procession re-entered the nave for the distribution while singing "All glory, laud, and honor." Leading the procession was an adult thurifer, followed by three children, one serving as crucifer, the other two as torchbearers, then the choir and clergy, followed inexplicably by about twelve children mismatched in size, age, gait, and dress and lending a ragtag aspect to the endeavor. A wary look around at the congregation revealed another dozen youngsters sporting T-shirts with pithy sayings, leather jackets, and docksiders *sans* socks—enough to give an oldtimer a start! The bulk of the congregation was made up of white women (45) and men (31), black women (10) and men (4), and one Indian man. Counting the choir (13), the ministers of the Mass (5), one female lector, three ushers, and a group of children that came and went (to Sunday School, presumably) (11), the total came to 124, about one-third the attendance 25-30 years earlier. The average age of the adults was about 40.

The sermon was delivered from notes in just over seven minutes from a lectern attached to the front pew, by the Curate, a tall, unmarried woman in her thirties. She described the season as the beginning of the end and the beginning of the beginning and accused us all of lacking ultimate values. She said the people in Jesus's time could not "tailor Him to their model," and neither can we. If we are truly Christian, we must suffer in some of the ways Christ suffered. We too can be rejected by friends. Like Christ, we often wonder why God seems to have deserted us. We must walk alone and uncertainly, like our Savior, trusting in the Father and watching and waiting with Christ in His agony.

The rector celebrated, clad in a chasuble, assisted by an older male priest as deacon in dalmatic and the Curate as subdeacon in tunicle. A newly ordained, unmarried, male deacon vested in a cinctureless alb participated from the bottom step.

In a conversation with the rector, an unmarried man in his early forties, at the coffee hour it was learned the congregation numbered about 700, with a median income of $10,000. He stated that the "old guard" (among them, seven millionaires) had died or been cleared out, that they were "falsely sophisticated," "without substance," and tried to "run the parish." When questioned about the presence of a female priest on the staff, the rector averred they "had to stay with the times." The writer was curious what one called such a priest here. "Anything she wants," he said, adding, "but don't call her Mother. She's nobody's mother, and I'm nobody's father. Call 'em all Presbyter." He went on to say that the church no longer looked to Nashotah House for clergy, that that seminary was "full of boneheads." He volunteered that he had "strong opinions" and, "as an intellectual with a doctorate and as a member of an old family from northern Virginia [was] more of an aristocrat than anyone who had ever been in the parish."

Suddenly, the Collect for the Day came to the writer's mind: "...all mankind should follow the example of [Christ's] great humility ..."

In an article for the August 2-9, 1989 issue of the *Christian Century*, entitled "The Episcopal Synod: Reinforcing Boundaries," William L. Sachs makes an interesting observation: "Fort Worth unwittingly marked the dissolution of the Anglo-Catholic party — a party that had won its place in the Episcopal Church. The irony, for those at Fort Worth, is that many of the Episcopal priests who now celebrate sung Eucharists in albs and chasubles are women, and that many of the male clergy who respect Anglo-Catholicism also applaud the consecration of a woman bishop. This leaves those who gathered at Fort Worth with only a retrospective sense of purpose. Being obsessed with boundaries rather than a vision of the larger church, they can only be a limited enclave."

I reject this analysis. Anglo-Catholic parishes have always appealed to a broad spectrum of life. They have not rejected minorities or those of deviant sexual practices, and the rich and the influential have been content to join in worship with everybody. What is happening is this: Those male priests singing the Eucharist who allegedly approve of female clergy are not approving ECUSA's policies; they have their own agenda — the sheltering of homosexuals. The irony is that they do not have to do so, for neither the Anglo-Catholic faction nor society as a whole any longer rejects them.

The liberalizing of the church is a reflection of the liberalizing of American society. For the clergy, as for the people at large, many actions heretofore discouraged or disallowed are now sanctioned. They include divorce, expressions of hetero- and homosexual freedom, civil disobedience, alleged ecclesiastical heresies, outspoken criticism of government policy, vigorous self-advancement, resistance to self-criticism, and the destruction of self-possessed totems (but not those of others). To the extent that counterforces of comparable gravity and importunity impinge upon this list we are not to take it as all bad. However, the way has been cleared of traditions interfering with the engineering of society along pragmatic secular lines. The church has become an industry responding to the demands of society. Its segments can be regrouped very much like a domestic automobile company in partnership with a Japanese firm or a television network acquiring a publishing business or ten companies forming a conglomerate. Its clergy have begun to think corporately. The people understand all this very well. After all, we are all human.

A fictional interlude:
THE FISHERMAN

The Rev. Peter C. Simonson cast his line over the side of the rowboat, toward the tree-lined lake shore, where the water was shallower, and waited. He had been doing this for much of the afternoon. It mattered little to him that he had caught nothing. For most of his life he had gone fishing when he needed to think. He always said, more seriously than jocularly, that particular activity afforded him the most efficacious exposure to the four elements: he sat upon water, fresh air was all about him, the good earth was always in sight, and the fire of his cigarette completed the atmosphere necessary to his ruminations.

This afternoon the formula was not working. But, he had to admit, his problems were greater than usual. Ever since he had walked out on his first wife ten years ago, after he had discovered her affair with an artist from the local college, his professional movement had been inexorably downward even though he had felt his emotional state had initially soared. Now both his status and his emotions had reached their nadir.

Lately, he had been perplexed by his mental state. No doubt, a part of his befuddlement was due to his second wife's walking out on him for "reasons of incompatibility." At the divorce trial she had called him, among other things, "an insincere religious fanatic." Traumatic as that situation had been, it did not, however, explain the worrisome little things that beset him these days and made up the bulk of his psychic distress. He had trouble remembering where he had laid his pen; he could not rely on his memory to guide him through a sermon anecdote; he kept hearing noises in the house at night even after he proved to himself they did not exist; he attached a dread to the prospect of taking even a short trip; and, many times a day he calculated his life expectancy by statistical and more arcane means.

What worried him most, though, was the paranoia he was developing. Although the people in his church had asserted again and again, individually and as a group, that they understood why his two marriages had broken up and that they did not judge him, he saw them talking among themselves and looking cautiously his way, and he knew they were plotting to have him removed from his pastorate. Quite by accident, he had heard one of his most influential parishioners say to the church secretary in regard to the associate pastor: "You know, sometimes I think John is a better preacher than Peter. An effective man in other ways, too. He's going to go places." Just the other day the secretary had hurriedly and surreptitiously scraped several letters off her desk into a trash bag which she then tied up and carried out for burning. The pullulation of his suspicions had, of late, overwhelmed him, and he sometimes found himself, to his horror, standing behind cracked doors listening to the conversation within. He would get to his office earlier than usual and rummage about his secretary's desk for evidence of his overthrow. When he heard the telephone ring, he would not wait for his buzzer, but would pick up the extension in the hope of catching someone off guard.

What is wrong with me? he thought. Am I going round the bend?

An ordinary person with his complaints might see a counselor. But his pride would not allow him to do that. After all, *he* was a counselor *par excellence*. People came to *him* for advice in such circumstances. Never one to make close friends — he often rationalized that he could not do so because of his position as leader of the flock — there was no one at all to turn to.

Why not try God, he wondered. Then he laughed at himself. Indeed! Why *not* try God! He *worked* for God. Then, too, that's the step he would recommend to a parishioner seeking assistance.

But what if God was not on his side? Maybe God had set his congregation against him. He couldn't fight down in his mind the recurring cliche: Physician, heal thyself! Upon reflection, though, his good sense — what was left of it, that is, he thought — told him he was not a "real" physician, for his healing ability was not so much a function of his expertise as of that divine power he invoked. He had to link up with God to acquire potency.

From earliest childhood it had been drilled into him that prayer works. He was sure he sensed its magic in the nursery rhyme: "Now I lay me down to sleep, I pray the Lord my soul to keep; If I should die before I wake, I pray the Lord my soul to take." As he grew a little older, he concluded that he was actually preserving his life by his perfunctory nightly recitation of this verse; it would be mortally dangerous not to say his prayers. As he grew still older, he saw the little prayer as treacherously sweet and containing a frightening element of diabolism. By the time he reached adulthood he had given up praying altogether, for, as he admitted to himself, he never got any real answers, just silence or an echo of his own voice or thoughts. His observation so unnerved him that he rationalized: If prayer is answered, it is no longer prayer but a conversation.

He observed lots of others who abjured prayer and whose lives prospered in all ways. He also encountered plenty of people who prayed their knees off and fell ill and died or were struck by lightning or a train. But because there were a few who prayed and seemed to demonstrate positive results, he retained a modicum of belief in the efficacy of prayer, enough so that he could recommend it to those seeking his counsel. He did not like his lukewarm attitude toward prayer, but he could not help the way he felt. He had never had a religious experience which became a central focus of his life.

He was honest enough to recognize that for some people religion is an indifferent thing, for others a life-overwhelming thing. For himself, it was little more than a formal and compartmental interest. Sometimes, he thought, he wore his religion like a mackintosh protecting him from God and man.

He glanced at his float; it sat motionless on the quiet surface. He laid his rod down in the length of the boat and, hands clasped and wrists on his knees, he bent his head over. For several minutes he maintained this posture, trying to decide what to do next. I must seek guidance, I must pray, he thought.

In his denomination it was not seemly to appear too pious. People did not kneel to pray; they did not clasp hands in a prayerful attitude. Such actions were disrespectful of man. But to stand was disrespectful of God, never mind that he knew it too was a hallowed attitude of prayer. What was left? You could legitimately pray lying down, he supposed, if you were about to go to sleep. Best of all to sit, he concluded, especially if you bowed your head just a bit. Yes, that is the proper prayer attitude because it contains just the right proportion of concession to God and man.

The minister began: "Oh, Lord," and paused for a moment to collect his thoughts and, in his best pulpit manner, continued: "I beseech thee for thy help." At that moment, what must have been an enormous bass gave a mighty tug on the line and caused the reel to pay out line with a sharp, ratchety warning sound. As the fisherman automatically leaned forward to arrest the travel of the line with the click stop, he lost his balance and pitched forward on his knees. At that very instant a voice from over the water in the direction of the shore called out of the gathering dusk: "Do you need help?"

It was perceived by the minister as a hollow-sounding, echo-like voice that enunciated only the words: ..."need help?" – the voice of God.

As he scrambled to his feet to respond to his Master, the boat skittered out from under the feet of this man of God. "Oh, yes," he cried as he plunged deeper into the lake, choking on the water and his tears, while the voice, now more desperate, continued to echo its offer of help.

E. Laity

For our discussion purposes a layman (or laywoman) is a communicant of the age of majority, not merely a baptized adult. This is admittedly a bit arbitrary, for membership statistics rely sometimes on the number of confirmed members (regardless of age), sometimes on the number of baptized, and sometimes on both, but in order to participate fully in all aspects of a parish a person must be baptized and confirmed and old enough legally to hold certain offices and provide certain functions. We are, of course, talking here about the Episcopal Church in the U.S.A., not about the Church of England or other provinces where the fact of establishment often confuses the issue.

The figures contained in the *1989 Episcopal Church Annual* begin with the year 1850, in which the church had a total of 89,359 communicants, baptized members not being counted at that time. It was not until 1930 that both means of tallying were listed: 1,939,453 baptized members and 1,287,431 communicants. From that year through 1985 (the latest year for which statistics are available) both categories are always given, together with a breakdown of domestic and overseas membership. Through 1968, the peak year, there is a steady increase in baptized and communicant membership with totals for that year as follows: 3,588,435 baptized members and 2,341,861 communicants. From that point on, though, there is a gradual drop in both categories, with the following totals for 1985: 2,972,607 baptized members and 1,963,625 communicants. The Prayer Book Society has provided more recent figures, which, sadly, continue to reflect the downward trend: Baptized members for 1986 — 2,504,507; for 1987 — 2,462,300.

It is not our intention here to suggest all the reasons why, in view of an exponentially growing population, there should be a decrease, rather than an increase in membership. However, considering the social turmoil beginning in 1968 and continuing well into the 1970's, two of the reasons must lie in a growing general secularization and in dissatisfaction with the church's role in society. That discontent has undoubtedly found expression among people who leave or do not join because they maintain the church has done too little to further their social agenda, and among people who withhold their support because they think the church has done too little to preserve its true nature. At least for the latter group, it is not a matter of "damned if you do, and damned if you don't"; it is a matter of selectivity of emphasis and of balance. But the Church gets hit from both directions, anyhow.

It used to be that selectivity of emphasis, say, on mission work at home or abroad, on church construction, on schools, the church's relationship to government, even racial matters, could be controlled by the laity and clergy working independently. Sometimes they would join forces, but it was seldom necessary. In fact, most of such matters were influenced far more by the attitude of the laity than of the clergy. A balance usually resulted because the clergy took a more conservative position and acted as a curb against the enthusiasms of the laity in and outside the church.

From the time of the civil rights movement in this country the clergy have taken a far more active stand in social matters than ever before. A sudden awareness of their power has led them into more and more daring adventures. They have swept along in their wake many of the laity who see the means of accomplishing many of their own personal or public objectives, such as rights for women and homosexuals, aid for the poor, the homeless, and the downtrodden, comfort to leftist governments, and church union schemes, to name a few. These actions have, for the first time, made allies of the clergy and the liberal lay element, a combination never imagined possible. The professional line separating the clergy from the laity has actually become so blurred that no one is any longer astonished at seeing clergy in their collars being carted off to jail or laymen giving their okay to doctrinal alterations they had been taught, by the clergy, to abhor.

In order to determine where the line-crossing occurs, if indeed at all, we need to list the traditional functions of the laity. Or perhaps a better way to establish the place of the laity is to indicate what the Church owes its members and what they owe their church.

The Church owes its laity an array of spiritual benefits. These include the sacraments in proper sequence; pastoral counseling and visitation in health, sickness of whatever sort, and death; Christian education, and participation in the worship and governance of the local and national church. It also owes its people the assurance that the Church knows its own mind, practices what it proclaims, guards its monetary resources, and defends its people in their assumptions of right belief. It should be unheard-of for the Church to vacillate in matters of faith, to do what it will not allow others to do, to spend money profligately or for projects bearing no fruit or inimical to the common or national good, and to ignore canon and constitutional law when it is advantageous to do so.

The laity owes the Church regular attendance at worship, money and service, recruitment of members, social outreach, and an understanding of and loyalty to the tenets of the Church.

The result of this implied social contract should ideally reflect a smoothly operating, intermeshing organization of bones and flesh, of structure and substance, of leadership and fellowship, of answers and questions and answers — not one of uncertainty and more uncertainty, of self-serving interests of the broadest *and* narrowest sort, and of statements which underlie neither questions nor answers of substance.

What has gone wrong in this arrangement is that the Church has not been entirely faithful to its laity's expectations. The laity in turn have failed in a task not traditionally theirs. They have failed — out of ignorance, indifference, and self-serving interests of their own — to ride herd on the clergy. In fact, precisely when the interests of the two groups have coincided, the clergy and the laity have forsaken their separate roles and joined forces. The problem is that that area of cooperation has been in matters normally considered professional clerical affairs. Who ever would have thought laymen would support, with talent and money, a barely visible group of clergy intent on creating a superchurch at the expense of hallowed beliefs? Who ever would have imagined that a social issue of the elastic magnitude of women's liberation would rewrite canon law without a pen and overturn a system of polity based on two thousand years of tradition? There is perhaps more excuse for inadvertently permitting theological changes in Prayer Book language.

The largest portion of the Church is made up of the laity. In democratic terms they should then have the greatest say in the governance of the Church. But, as we well know, the Church is set up to receive that input from the laity that tends to further the objectives of the clergy. If the objectives of the clergy, independently arrived at by them, happen to coincide with the goals of the laity, then all is well.

In recent years, the goals have been identical, but for different reasons. Where the male clergy have given their consent to the ordination of females, it has been in response to the pressure of society. It certainly could not have been because they were eager to welcome double their number in the priesthood to fight for the same number of jobs! Women among the laity lobbied for admission to the priesthood because many felt genuinely called, some had an axe to grind, some were seeking the same hiding place from worldly pressures that their male counterparts have always sought, many came from Rome because they saw no hope there, and many more were the result of broken marriages and homosexual relationships.

The revision of the 1928 Prayer Book was at first vigorously resisted by the laity, but when the people realized they did not possess the claim to expertise in such matters, they backed off. The relatively few clergy who did resist were drowned out by cacophonous counter-voices proclaiming progress, innovation, new insights, harmony, etc. Two things then happened to the laity: They began to *forget* their objections to a revision —

and simultaneously to become used to the new version of the Prayer Book—and they saw an opportunity to appear liberal and understanding—a time-honored characteristic of the ideal Christian life—by accepting a new book to the exclusion of all other options.

Already the long-term presence of COCU had caused most people to become dulled to its effects; in a word, they had here too *forgotten* what it was they should object to. Besides, to object loudly—even authoritatively—to something that advertized "a greater good" was almost un-American. The clergy saw an opportunity to bolster their sagging numbers by becoming a part of a larger group; they either subscribed to the process or did not object to it.

The Episcopal laity are of three types. The first group, probably now the smallest, are those born into the Church who have remained convinced and committed Episcopalians. Their activities include decent service to the Church; their convictions are based as much on familiarity with the Church and its attendant status as on knowledge of the current problems in the Church. Then there are those who might be called nominal Episcopalians, those who readily characterize themselves as Churchmen but who attend services only rarely, who make their Easter obligation and little more. They are among the first who assert their rights to Baptism, Confirmation, Matrimony, and the last rites. There are, in addition, those who are converts from other faiths and who constitute the largest number and most active group of Episcopalians. That group is comprised of those who are willing to accept whatever steps are taken by the Church to amalgamate the Church's beliefs with those of other non-Roman denominations, and those who converted for very specific reasons and who are not willing to compromise under any circumstances.

The first group squeaks its objections to new trends occasionally, but not forcefully; the second group joins them. The liberal wing of the third group reacts in silence to every innovation; the conservative wing makes a great deal of noise, but is never heard. In his address before the General Convention in Detroit in 1988 Presiding Bishop Edmond Browning coldly proclaimed his willingness to bid "Godspeed" to all those who do not agree with the Church's policies. However, in response to the meeting in June 1989 of the Fort Worth Synod, called by the Evangelical and Catholic Mission and at which two thousand Episcopalians and twenty-two sympathetic bishops gathered to protest the extreme and radical actions of the Church, Bishop Browning gave this baffling statement: "I cannot overemphasize my belief that those who disagree with the majority must not be marginalized [*sic*] in our Church and will not be. This is not a political strategy. This is a theological necessity." In an article in *Forward Day by Day* Bishop Browning further states: "We are not in a position to decide whether or not we wish to be inclusive: we *are* inclusive, blessedly so! Our church is one in which people who disagree passionately — about things which matter greatly — can share the Body and Blood of the Christ who died *for all* and made no exceptions. ... I have occasion — fairly often — to plead for this idea. I cannot think of anything that lies so close to my heart. In church life, in personal life, in any kind of life in Christ, there can be no outcasts."[24]

But the bishop's words belie his actions. He has not bemoaned our deviations from the Chicago Quadrilateral; he has not questioned the objectives of COCU; he has not spoken out clearly on homosexual priests; he has not given public evidence of understanding the "Continuing Church" movement; and he has only a tenuous grip on the loyalties of the Prayer Book Society and the new Synod. In August 1990 Bishop Browning rebuked the Prayer Book Society for "harassing" Bishop Spong for his having ordained a practicing homosexual, and in September 1990 the Presiding Bishop ignored a petition on prayer-book choice signed by 11,293 loyal Episcopalians. Let us not forget, this is our chief shepherd who at General Convention in Detroit bid "Godspeed" to dissenters, when he should have been assiduously striving to keep them.

Should the dissenters be taken seriously?

They are part of the problem and the solution.

CHAPTER VII

Solutions

"We have not so much as heard whether there be any Holy Ghost."

—*Acts 19:2*

"Answer not a fool according to his folly, lest thou also be like unto him. Answer a fool according to his folly, lest he be wise in his own conceit."

—*Proverbs 26:4-5*

A. Farewell to the Holy Ghost?

The Holy Ghost is hard to pin down theologically. Often defined as that aspect of the Christian God immanent in this world, He has typically been considered a paraclete or intercessor, a comforter or strengthener. The principal reference in the Bible to the Holy Ghost is found in John 14:16, where Christ is speaking to his disciples: "And I will pray the Father, and he shall give you another Comforter, that he may abide with you for ever." In verse 18, Christ adds: "I will not leave you comfortless: I will come to you." The other reference to the Holy Ghost, the recounting of His manifestation to the apostles, is found in Acts 2:1-4: "And when the day of Pentecost was fully come, they were all with one accord in one place. And suddenly there came a sound from heaven as of a rushing mighty wind, and it filled all the house where they were sitting. And there appeared unto them cloven tongues like as of fire, and it sat upon each of them. And they were all filled with the Holy Ghost, and began to speak with other tongues, as the Spirit gave them utterance."

Since the Holy Ghost is the third Person of the Trinity, there is always the risk of blasphemy in suggesting that He depart from the scene. But there is an equal risk of blasphemy in insisting, as many have done, that He has directed an operation for which an airtight excuse is needed to offset criticism and uncertainty. The Holy Ghost is not a supernatural force waiting to be summoned to do the bidding of men and women; the grace of God, through the Holy Ghost, comes to us as a gift. The Holy Ghost is the infusement of God Himself and Christ Himself; His presence in this life is the expression of their will. One does not quickly announce that the Holy Ghost was responsible for any given action. That is a pompous assertion.

Furthermore, a study of history often proves it was not the Holy Ghost after all that effected this or that change, for in the perspective of time the change has been reevaluated and seen as undesirable. Therefore, it cannot be said at this juncture that permitting women to be ordained was a clear blessing received from the Holy Ghost. In plain English, it seems now it may have been a dire mistake to ordain women to the diaconate *at that time*. And it was an enlargement of that initial mistake to proceed with ordinations through the episcopal level. Appeals to the Holy Ghost (or to "God's will") are too often invalidated by subsequent history. That fellowship, that unity of spirit, engendered by the Holy Ghost and by which the people of old were bound so strongly that no divisive elements in their Christian experience could pull them apart, is now rent asunder. It would have been better to wait, to proceed more deliberately.

In a long pastoral letter written during the spring of 1989, and before the Fort Worth synod, Presiding Bishop Browning states: "What we have in common is more important than what divides. We dare not now lose that which has been purchased at so high a price. We dare not now squander that for which the martyrs and saints have struggled so painfully." He forthrightly puts himself in company with the martyrs and saints and gives tacit approval to division, yet all the while failing to define the common ground to which he refers. Is it not rather obviously the threefold ministry within the apostolic tradition as practiced by the historic Catholic Communions? He chooses as his text Ephesians 4:2-3: "Be humble always and gentle, and patient too. Be forbearing with one another and charitable. Spare no effort to make fast with bonds of peace the unity which the Spirit gives."

What to do? Shouldn't a religious organization, a church, feel free to assert that the Holy Ghost was responsible for some desired action?

No, not simultaneously with the undertaking of that action.

Why?

It misleads and subtly coerces people into believing something that may in fact not be true. It also implies that the Church can manipulate God. And, furthermore, it bespeaks an infallibility of the people — usually the clergy, and among them, usually the bishops.

What to do? First, behave rationally and pragmatically, and remember, as the 1928 Book of Common Prayer tells us in the Offices of Instruction (p.285), that the work of the Holy Ghost is to "sanctify . . . *all* [italics mine] the people of God." What the Holy Ghost does is not necessarily democratic; it is not a majority vote of the moment; it is a confirmation of the tradition of the Church throughout its history.

To the bishops we would say: Humility and charity begin at home.

B. Schism as Alternative

The Synod in Fort Worth had as their purpose in meeting "to determine how the Evangelical and Catholic Mission (ECM) shall be the Church within the Episcopal Church and to adopt a detailed and unified plan for active witness in the face of the institution's present disintegration." For ECUSA this was schismatic talk, although a careful reading of the above statement indicates a willingness on the part of the ECM to remain "within the Episcopal Church."

From June 1-3, 1989, the Episcopal Synod of America met as a group of two thousand parish representatives and twenty-two ECUSA bishops, together with the Bishop of London, and bishops from Africa, Australia, Scotland, South America, and the South Pacific. The group devised its own "interim" constitution and established "areas" in the continental United States to be "served" by six dioceses set up by the synod. This move, in effect, was taken to allow the synod to function semiautonomously and to hold fast to those traditions it considers essential to maintaining the true Catholicity of the Church. Traditionalist parishes could then request an "episcopal visitor" from among the synod's bishops to perform ministrations in a way agreeable to them and without taint of performance by a female bishop. The Bishop of Fort Worth, Clarence Pope, who also serves as President of the Synod, has argued that this approach "would meet all needs without disturbing jurisdictional boundaries of any diocese or violating the constitution and canons of the Episcopal Church." Needless to say, most bishops of ECUSA find this arrangement unacceptable; for them their dioceses are inviolable territory.

Bishop William Wantland of Eau Claire disagrees. A lawyer before ordination, he insists that precedents have already been established, for dioceses have long cooperated with each other in various programs, in financial matters, and when in general need of mutual support. Bishops have customarily been free to operate in dioceses other than their own as long as the parish clergy have invited them, usually, though not always, with the consent of the diocesan. No change in church law has resulted from such typically ad hoc visits, and none should be contemplated now. It is all quite legal.

It is worth noting that the Church's 1988 General Convention did in fact endorse the use of "episcopal visitors" as a move to pacify that element of the Church in opposition to the ordination of women. But the Anglican primates meeting in Cyprus in May 1989 roundly rejected the idea as incorporating the danger of "parallel jurisdictions." In their heart of hearts all the bishops see the plan for what it is: an alternative to schism.

It will be interesting to see what the standoff produces. The lines have been drawn. The liberal ECUSA bishops feel their prerogatives are being threatened by the possible incursion of bishops from outside their bailiwick. No one likes to lose power and influence, and that is what they fear more than the dissolution of the national church. The traditionalist bishops are, admittedly, also seeking power and influence — however, not through change, but through retention of the Church's longstanding principles. One distressing fact stands out. Liberality no longer means toleration of disparate views; it has taken on a totalitarian aspect in violation of the word's definition. Being "liberal" means being illiberal. Do it our way or move aside.

One of these days a test case will strain the fabric of the Episcopal Church. Some Synod bishop is going to enter a diocese not his own at the request of a parish, and the fat will be in the fire. The diocesan will order the extraneous bishop out; the bishop will refuse to forego his ministrations. The parish will defend him; the Synod will defend him; ECUSA will support the diocesan. The

Synod will meet and threaten to withdraw from the Church. Peace will be made. It will happen again. Peace may not follow this time.

Do the traditionalists have enough strength to back up their threats of schism? At the Fort Worth gathering were not only twenty retired bishops but six active ones along with nine from overseas, including Bishop Graham Leonard from the prestigious diocese of London next door to Canterbury. There are almost three hundred traditionalist parishes in eighty-six of the ninety-five U.S. dioceses, and the number is growing. These same bishops and parishioners and priests approaching fourteen thousand have already signed the Synod's Declaration of Common Faith and Purpose, and the Synod is striking for 200,000 signatures by Christmas of 1990.

What would schism entail? First of all, there would be immediate spiritual damage to a formerly united church, and the heartache would be experienced in both the liberal and the conservative camps. There would follow legal entanglements over ownership of church property. An enormous loss of funds for the present national church would result. There would be initial confusion of relationship with the wider Anglican Communion. Many COCU objectives would be thwarted. The outlook of the Church of England toward many incipient innovations might be fortified. Ecumenical relations with Rome and Orthodoxy would definitely be affected positively. How many of these are worthwhile outcomes? Different answers will come from different sides. But what if it all leads to a healthier unity? Would it then not be a salutary step?

Is there a way of avoiding the uncertain results of a schism? I think there is. If many of the three hundred traditionalist parishes were to withhold their financial support to their dioceses *or to their own parishes* for only a short while, say, six months or a year, the hierarchy would begin to listen because money talks with a loud voice. With such an example of commitment before the church at large, no hierarchy in its right mind is going to risk having other parishes follow their lead. Capitulation will result. And it can be conveniently rationalized as a return to old principles.

C. Pan-Protestantism

It all really got started during the first decade of this century. Many Protestants seemed to notice for the first time that there was great diversity within their ranks, yet some suspected there might be a basis for a kind of cooperation, if not unity. After all, many reasoned that, despite the obvious differences, there had to be some underlying agreement in doctrine. If nothing else, everybody accepted Jesus as the Christ and everybody recognized the two major sacraments of Baptism and Holy Communion.

The Foreign Missions Conference of North America was the first effective group to cross Protestant denominational lines, and in 1907 it achieved solid organizational status. Its objectives were modest by today's standards. Shying clear of theological divisions, it concentrated on practical goals, often in the name of more efficient functioning, not unlike businesses today which join together loosely to produce a single product, but the constituents of which are manufactured or refined by the individual companies.

In time, the Conference was emboldened to examine the divisive issues it had originally skirted and in 1910 gave birth to what was called the Faith and Order Movement of the Episcopal Church. The movement saw as its task the close examination of the doctrinal differences which had occasioned the denominational system, and it sought ways of achieving a new unity.

Simultaneous with these movements was another, created in 1908 and called the Federal Council of the Churches of Christ in America. The Council combined the objectives of functional cooperation and spiritual relationship among the member churches. It looked toward unity, but did not attempt to specify what shape the unified church might take nor when union might be accomplished. It is interesting that present-day union schemes still have not decided what form or forms unification among Protestant churches might assume. Part of the reason for lack of commitment to the ultimate shape stems from honest ignorance of what will work, and part is based on diplomatic caution that the incipient structure not come tumbling down before it is completely erected. Perhaps only Episcopal Bishop Charles H. Brent was convinced the individual churches should lose their identity. He managed to push through a resolution at General Convention in October 1910 inviting "all Christian communions throughout the world which confess Our Lord Jesus Christ as God and Saviour" to set up a conference "for the consideration of questions touching Faith and Order."

The immediate response was encouraging; some eighteen denominations expressed interest. But World War I intervened and inhibited progress. Overtures to churches overseas were made, including one to the Roman Catholic Church. Little that was concrete came of these early efforts, but interest in the idea never disappeared. Many at the grass roots level kept the movement alive. Their enthusiasm and persistence produced the community church, a phenomenon still with us in form and spirit. This kind of federated church constituted no break with the denominational system as such, but allowed members of two or more different denominations to come together in a single, denominationally undesignated local church. In the minds of many, this is the workable model for the future — pan-Protestantism in miniature. It was supported — particularly in the South — by interdenominational revivals held in tents, later in meeting halls, and now in civic centers and on television. Mass appeal and mass servicing. Is it any wonder that within non-Catholic churches people became less and less aware of crucial differences in their churches?

How often has the reader heard a fellow parishioner remark: "Raised in the Episcopal Church? Oh, no. We were raised Methodists. Ernest and I just like your service, and besides, we live close by."

There are many variations on this theme, but it is clear these people might just as well have been shopping for a motor company. It is not our place to judge Ernest and his wife, nor is it our duty to debate the advantages and disadvantages of Episcopalianism and Methodism; it is our task to delineate other conditions and attitudes that have led to such spiritual vacuity.

It probably could only happen in America. For one thing, the number of denominations here is still overwhelming. How can anyone remember all the subtle differences? How can one even remember the names of some churches? Listed in the fifth edition of the *Handbook of Denominations*, edited by Frank S. Mead, are, for example, 27 different kinds of Baptist churches, 22 Methodist churches, and 10 Presbyterian churches. There is the Church of God and the Church of God (Apostolic), The (Original) Church of God, Inc., the Church of God (Anderson, Indiana), the Church of God (Seventh Day), the Church of God and Saints of Christ, the Church of God by Faith, Inc., the Church of God in Christ, and the Worldwide Church of God.

If movement among these myriad sub-denominations is possible with impunity, it is not surprising that actual denominational lines are crossed all the time, for there are more than 250 denominations and sub-forms, and there are millions of people. Shifting is particularly prevalent among those who, for another thing, are in a church primarily for a social or business reason. Everyone knows the Episcopal Church occupies the highest rung on both the social and business ladders.

Pluralism among non-Catholic denominations is, to a large extent, a reflection of the freedom enjoyed by Americans to choose what suits them in every quarter of life. Without implying any cynicism, one can, after all, despite some social, racial, and ethnic restrictions, marry whom one wants, live where one wants, shop where one wishes, drive what and wherever one desires as long as one has the money. Why should there be any restrictions within churches?

In the last twenty years especially, many churches have had to face the corrosive effects of pluralism. Most of the barriers that differentiated one denomination from another at the beginning of the century have come down. The mobility of American society has thrust country people into cities, city people into the suburbs. Industry has moved people; people have moved themselves as they have gained in income. Ethnicity and regionalism have disappeared or been transformed into sentimental attachments. Some of these forces have, of course, been at work within Roman Catholicism, but by and large, the phenomenon has had a religious impact on Protestantism alone, where there is far less unity of belief. Whatever movement there has been *out of* Roman Catholicism has been for reasons of indifference toward religion or pique toward Catholicism. The movement *into* any given Protestant denomination — and here we include the Episcopal Church — has been based on indifference toward individual church tenets or on a specific social objective. The result has been a general elimination of denominational differentiation, particularly within Protestantism, and a hazy line between religion and society. Fundamentalism is the only force to see itself in opposition to many secular practices of less than an idealistic nature.

Since there is a minimum of transfer between Roman and non-Roman churches, the mix of denominations is limited to intra-Protestant changes. If we rely on the continuing effectiveness of secular and religious forces presently at work in America, we can safely predict an amalgamation of first- and second-line Protestant churches, but excluding more than half of the eleven Lutheran bodies in the United States. Since the powerful and numerous Baptist churches, together with countless splinter groups, constitute the bulk of fundamentalist faiths, their amalgamation within Protestantism is somewhat problematic, more along cooperative than theological lines. But even with these conditions, the result will be a massive evangelical counterforce to traditional Christianity. It will not be a new Reformation by any means, for it represents not a breakaway based on theological differences — not an inimical action — but a boiling away or a boiling down based on indifferentism.[25]

Is this a sufficient or safe reason for seeking or allowing pan-Protestantism to take hold?

It is not, for indifferentism is inherently negative. Union cannot be allowed simply to happen. It must be approached aggressively, or it must be foregone. That visible unity of the Church which many faithful Christians have longed for must be founded upon the biblical notion of *all* the people of God. Three-quarters of the world's Christians reside in the Roman Catholic, Anglican, Orthodox, and Lutheran Communions. They cannot be ignored.

Neither does the Episcopal Church, as a member of the worldwide Anglican Communion, have the right to join the forces of indifferentism to the destruction of those doctrines that can form the basis for a holy union. The Episcopal Church, in its liberalism, is corporate evidence of the typical American insistence upon absolute freedom of action. In its cooperation — nay, its instigation of interaction and union — with Protestant bodies, the Episcopal Church ignores its relationship and responsibility to worldwide Anglicanism. By its actions it has identified itself almost exclusively with Protestantism, while proclaiming in a whisper that it also subscribes to the full and ancient Catholicity of the historic Church.

It is very difficult to see how one can have it both ways, at least at this time. The Episcopal Church is bargaining away — to what ends? — its special identity. Very soon it will have no bargaining power whatsoever, either with the Protestants, who will have taken from it what they needed, or with the Catholic world, who cannot accept it in its adulterated form. It will therefore have to suffer dissolution in the Protestant world or be swallowed up by Rome under her conditions. Pun intended, the Episcopal Church is now between a hard place and a Rock.

I have no doubt it will choose the hard place of Protestant anonymity. For several days beginning at the end of September 1989, Archbishop of Canterbury Robert Runcie paid a visit to Pope John Paul II in the Vatican for the purpose of discussing the eventual reuniting of the two communions. Runcie is the fourth Archbishop of Canterbury since 1960 to make the trip to Vatican City and embrace a pope. It did not go down well with British evangelicals who inalterably oppose any overtures to Rome. The Rev. Ian Paisley of Northern Ireland, head of the anti-Catholic Free Presbyterian Church there, threatened repeatedly to disrupt the Archbishop's four-day meeting.

Paisley and other evangelicals were particularly upset when Archbishop Runcie called on all Christians to accept the pope as a common leader "presiding in love." Runcie said, "For the universal church, I renew the plea: Could not all Christians come to reconsider the kind of primacy the bishop of Rome exercised within the early church, a 'presiding in love' for the sake of the unity of the churches in the diversity of their mission?" Beside himself with rage, Paisley answered for himself and millions, "This is high treason!" At an Anglican service at All Saints Church, at which Vatican officials were present, three of Paisley's clerical associates jumped up just before the Archbishop's sermon and ripped off their jackets, displaying T-shirts emblazoned with "Runcie is a traitor to Protestant Britain" and "Remember Cranmer." (Cranmer was the first Archbishop of Canterbury. He was burned at the stake by Roman Catholics for his Protestant ideas.)

Archbishop Runcie has defended his view on the role of the pope. He claimed he had not meant that the pope should interfere in the affairs of the Anglican Church, and certainly not in the British government, the latter statement in answer to those who had criticized him for "subverting the British Constitution." He explained: "The phrase 'universal primacy' has a spiritual meaning. It does not imply political supremacy and does not suggest that the pope should administer the affairs of the Church of England."

The Protestants have nothing to fear. The very fact that these friendly encounters between Rome and Canterbury have been going on for years without any tangible union results is proof enough for most people that Rome is not really interested. The impediments to union have always been numerous and profound, but now, as Pope John Paul himself makes clear, they are, to all intents and purposes, prohibitive: "As we meet today, we cannot but acknowledge that events in recent years have seriously aggravated the differences between us, making the work of the commission [reference is to a commission created in 1982 to study designing a theological framework for unity] more difficult. The ordaining of women effectively blocks the path to the mutual recognition of ministries." With such a promise from the pope there is little chance the Church of England will now continue to resist the ordination of women. The Protestant element inside and outside the Church of England will buy the safest insurance policy in the world and lobby vigorously for female ordination.

Aside from a loss of individual church theology, pan-Protestantism will produce an organization large enough to combat or infect Rome, *but only in the United States* — and resistance to Rome must be one of the major unverbalized goals of the arrangement. By participating in Protestant union schemes, the Episcopal Church may — even in its resulting anonymity — be able to fight Rome more effectively, but at the same time it will disrupt, demoralize, and destroy its sister churches within the Anglican Communion.

D. What Role Ecumenism?

Strange as it may seem, the discussion can begin at the time of the Reformation, a period of rancor, disruption, and outright schism. At the outset, the Reformation seemingly represented everything diametrically opposed to union, yet it carried in it the seeds of reunion. The number of autonomous units resulting from the Reformation is in the thousands. This fact alone persuades many that Protestantism fosters at its core some inexplicable divisive principle that propels it to disintegration. Protestants themselves rather proudly maintain and explain that this feature is a reflection of their unqualified individualism. Some Protestants are embarrassed by all the splintering; others are, frankly, dismayed because they believe the Church of Luther had no intention of departing from the essentials of the Holy Catholic Church. In any event, whatever tension existed in those early post-Reformation days between the desire to break away and the desire to remain a part of the historic Church was minimal in comparison with that of later years. From the very start, Martin Luther himself sought change and renewal within the Church, not disruption. At no time did Luther or any of his followers repudiate the historic creeds, nor did they reject any doctrines formulated on them.

An examination of the other side — that of the Roman Church — reveals a similar, remarkable disposition to preserve and conserve and not to tear down. Surely, the most irenic figure in all this was Desiderius Erasmus of Rotterdam. Of course, some will immediately say that Rome had more to lose than the adherents of Luther. True though that may be in material terms, it is certainly not true in spiritual terms; and both sides recognized this fact.

The opposition hardened only gradually until it reached the rigid state of the last hundred years. From the point of view of the Protestants, the reasons are many, but several stand out. First, by fragmenting, the Protestants lost their single voice and effective combined strength to confront and bargain with Rome. Secondly, Rome's control of governments led to distasteful confrontations on a non-religious plane. Thirdly, the pope himself presented peculiar problems, but the one that soared above all others was his proclaimed infallibility in matters of faith and morals and the pronouncements that followed that alleged attribute. From the Catholic viewpoint, those outside "the true Church" were heretics — and that pretty much ended the matter. If there was to be any reunion, it had to be on Rome's terms — which meant, simply, no deal.

Today, words such as heretic and schismatic are out of vogue, to put it mildly. Not that people don't think they know a heretic or a schismatic when they see one; it is just not nice to call someone such things. One euphemism that passes muster is "separated brethren." (The implication is still "separated from the true Church.") Mostly, people today avoid the whole matter of labels and resort to two big categories: Protestants and Catholics.

This categorization of Christianity—note that the Orthodox have been overlooked—suits Rome just fine. This way they do not have to deal with "separated brethren" on more than one level and can effectively ignore the claims of Canterbury or any other church in the apostolic succession. The Orthodox are not actually in the same hopper; they are less offensive to Rome theologically but are equally deserving of Rome's suspicion because of a peculiar history of mutual animosity. (Another example where religion divides.)

Luther saw the Church as wider than the Church of Rome. He recognized many Christian bodies as part of the universal Church even though they were not in communion with Rome. He heatedly made this assertion in the Leipzig Disputation of 1519 with the Catholic theologian Johann Meier von Eck. The latter's high regard for the papacy prompted Luther to refer to "the many thousands of saints" of the Greek Church not under the pope's control. The Reformers viewed the Orthodox Church favorably and hoped for their Eastern brethren's support in the conflict with Rome. Luther insisted that his stance was more Christian, more Catholic, and more ecumenical than Eck's.

Today, ecumenism is not argued out publicly and finally by single prominent theologians in the Protestant and Roman Catholic camps. Instead, there are isolated voices from both sides, carrying little authority except where the utterance is from the Roman Magisterium. Not even the Archbishop of Canterbury wields the authority in his own Communion that one might well expect. It all appears to be mere groundwork.

At their meeting in September 1989 Archbishop Robert Runcie and Pope John Paul II signed a document aimed at repairing the centuries-old split between their Communions. It read in part: "We here solemnly recommit ourselves and those we represent to the restoration of visible unity and full ecclesial communion." The Archbishop commented, "I'm full of hope that we shall be able to build on the understanding and unity which we already enjoy between the Anglican and Catholic Church." But the document continued, as we have already indicated in an earlier section, with the cautionary statement that "the ordination of women prevents reconciliation between us even where there is otherwise progress toward agreement."

In the impatience of modern times, particularly in America, such conversations ought to be cause for despair. Something must be wrong with the whole approach to ecumenism. This is not to imply that it is a simple matter that can be easily fixed. If church unity is a desirable goal — and this is a moot question to be examined further in the next section — all avenues are worth exploring.

As in friendship or marriage, each party must bring something worthwhile to the relationship. Like business, the Church must have a product to sell to ready consumers. Like the military, or countries facing each other down, churches must have sufficient power to deal with the adversary. Like any one-to-one relationship, the one with more power calls the shots. One is reminded of Thrasymachus's observation in *The Republic*: "What I say is that 'just' or 'right' means nothing but what is to the interest of the stronger party." The resulting relationship may be the better or the worse for both parties; it is a gamble. If there is equal power between two forces, there is a standoff, a stalemate, or gradual mutual disintegration of purpose.

It is fair to say that at the moment no real relationship exists between Rome and the Protestant and/or Anglican world. Rome's numbers alone overwhelm the "opposition." With approximately 952 million Roman Catholics worldwide, the piddling 70 million Anglicans and 338 million assorted Protestants hardly pose a threat (all figures are 1988 counts as reported by the *World Christian Encyclopedia* for the 1989 *Encyclopedia Britannica*). (The figure for Orthodox Christianity is 162 million.) And this is all the more true because both the Anglicans and the Protestants are divided, respectively, into autonomous bodies and sects. Furthermore, there is no head among the latter groups comparable in authority to the pope, no one who can emphatically and bindingly speak for a large mass of people — not even the Archbishop of Canterbury, the prelate of greatest stature in the Western Church outside Rome. Aside from altruistic motives — always suspect when issuing from a substantial power base — why would Rome bother to make overtures to a vast collection of denominations? Whom would they apply to in Western Christianity? Only the Archbishop of Canterbury qualifies, and we have already seen over a period of one hundred years — counting only somewhat arbitrarily from 1896 when Pope Leo XIII declared in the Bull *Apostolicae Curae* that Anglican orders were invalid — what foot-dragging there has been. The blunt fact is that Rome does not need Anglicanism or Protestantism.

Why does Anglicanism think it needs Protestantism? The question is put first this way because, as we have seen, it has been the Anglicans — more specifically, the American Episcopalians — who have taken the initial steps toward union and who doggedly hold on to their membership in union organizations.

There are several answers.

First of all, for good or for bad, Episcopalians are a national lot. They have always seen themselves as the American church. Their membership is the best-heeled, best-educated, and most vocal unified ecclesiastical throng. Their church is autonomous but the most significant constituent of the worldwide Anglican Communion. Despite the relative rigidity of their liturgy and doctrine, they are an exceedingly liberal bunch with a sense of social outreach.

Secondly, Episcopalians are largely converts from other faiths. They bring with them, of course, many treasures from their former church homes, but they also bring along subconsciously uncertainties based on memories. This breeds a kind of inner apologetic stance vis-a-vis other denominations. As one influential churchwoman recently told me when I tried to initiate a conversation about some of the problems facing the church: "I don't know anything about all that; I was raised a Methodist." Or another: "We did it [securing a new clergyman] differently in [again the Methodist Church] my childhood church." Still another: "The Presbyterians do a much better job of visiting than we do. I know because that's how I originally became a Presbyterian." Or an Episcopal priest, himself a convert, in regard to the reception of communion by an unconfirmed non-member: "It's the same God, isn't it?"

These memories surface also in statements of incredulity that Episcopalians can consider themselves Catholics. Many have never noticed that the Prayer Book uses the term priest when sacerdotal functions are called for. When this is pointed out, horror is often registered. There is, therefore, obvious resistance to using "Father" ("Mother" soon?) as a term of address even if the priest expresses his preference for it. In short, the Episcopal Church has more than a patina of Protestantism about it. Just think back no more than twenty-five years and recall the starkness of ceremonial in all but Anglo-Catholic parishes. The present "upgrading" in ceremonial is as much a result of general Protestant acceptance of collars, stoles, robes, albs, and even chasubles as it is of conviction on the part of Episcopalians. There is safety in numbers of like-minded people.

Thirdly, contrary to the prevalent opinion that, even if Episcopalians are politically and socially liberal, they are hidebound in their polity, the evidence shows a rebel tendency to disprove the notion. For a liberal diocese such as Massachusetts, the temptation to throw caution to the winds and elect a female bishop was just too great. The temptation to withdraw from the national church and form a new church may be too great one day for the leaders of the Fort Worth Synod.

Fourthly, the Episcopal Church possesses treasures not available to Protestantism, and instead of husbanding them—we will look at that possibility in the next section—the Church likes to "spend" its wealth. "Spending" (some would say "squandering") makes it look good and generous, not shriveled and miserly.

Fifthly, the Episcopal Church, like any organization, is composed of and run by individuals who have personal axes to grind. Many motives are born of sincere concern for the uniting of the Christian Church, but probably just as many involve goals of self-aggrandizement. I hope it is not cynical to ask what bishop would not like more influence and control. It is only human nature to seek power.

Why does Protestantism need Anglicanism?

Here, too, there are several answers. First, Protestantism is a faith of many pieces in dire need of a spokesman. It is not even a loose federation; it is a Humpty Dumpty presenting a reconstruction problem as difficult as rebuilding an egg. The Episcopal Church, with its polity and set liturgy, provides a public, authoritarian image and a model structure around which the various denominations can cluster. They do not emulate this image and this structure — else many problems would evanesce — but they use it as the most respectable front available.

Secondly, the structure of the Episcopal Church has something to *confer* upon the other churches should they desire it: a ministry unquestioned in the Protestant world, congregations of undoubted influence and wealth, a time-tested liturgy, and influence with Canterbury.

Thirdly, in its parish organization it possesses characteristics of many constituents of Protestantism: congregational control of most affairs, including the selection of a pastor; a variety of services; a commitment to outreach; emphasis on good Sunday School training and confirmation classes; a distrust of Rome; a distinct American coloration; little ethnicity.

If these two groups are such a good fit, why has it taken so long to effect a union? There are two reasons, one from each side. One, there are built-in brakes in the Episcopal Church preventing the loss of its peculiar nature. Two, there is a lingering suspicion on the part of some Protestants that the Episcopal Church does not know its own mind and that it will impose some of its Catholic traditions and an overdose of its upper-class mentality when no one is looking. This second misgiving is based primarily on the conditions that might be laid down about the acceptance of their diverse ministry and the necessity for re-ordination. The solution has been to wear down the opposition. In this the Protestants have been gradually successful.

In order to allay their residual suspicions of the Episcopal Church, the Protestant denominations need to confront the Episcopal Church with their own unified strength. If, then, a union can be effected between them and the Episcopal Church, the combined new church can use its greater strength in bargaining with Canterbury and Rome.

How can this be accomplished? Given the enormous number of Protestant bodies, it will not be easy. But there is a first step that can be taken.

Of those many Protestant denominations and sects, five mainline churches can be singled out as containing a substantial membership and being qualified to lead the pack in a novel endeavor. They are the Baptists, Lutherans, Methodists, Presbyterians, and the United Church of Christ. Each of these denominations, unlike the still generally unified Episcopalians, consists of a multitude of similar, though separate, groups still identifying themselves under the aegis of their denominational names. We proceed logically from the assumption that each of these groups contains sub-groups more similar to each other than to groups or sub-groups of any other denominational designation. For example, there is every reason to believe that the American Baptist Convention is more like the Southern Baptist Convention or the American Baptist Association or the Free Will Baptists or the General Baptists or the Regular Baptists or the Duck River Associations of Baptists or the Two-Seed-in-the-Spirit Predestinarian Baptists, etc. than Presbyterians of any stripe. There is equal reason to believe that the United Presbyterian Church in the U.S.A. is more like the Presbyterian Church in the United States or the Associate Presbyterian Church of North America or the Bible Presbyterian Church or the Second Cumberland Presbyterian Church in the United States, etc. than Baptists of any type. There are twenty-seven different kinds of Baptist churches and ten different Presbyterian bodies in the United States just as there are many different kinds of Lutherans, Methodists, and Congregationalists. All of these and the remaining 245-plus Protestant sects differ considerably from each other, and monumentally from the Episcopal Church. It therefore makes considerably more sense from every standpoint to expect these groups to unite *within themselves* before uniting with groups unlike themselves. The fact that they have not already been able to get together highlights the difficulties involved, but it also throws into bold perspective the futility of their uniting outside their denominational bounds.

What conceivable sense does it make for eight non-Episcopal churches, as subscribers to COCU, to pretend to join with the Episcopal Church when they represent not eight unified bodies but eight units out of a total of thirty-five? If the Presbyterian Church (USA) cannot combine with other Presbyterian bodies, if the United Methodist Church can only combine with the African Methodist Episcopal Church (AME), the African Methodist Episcopal Zion Church (AMEZ), and the Christian Methodist Episcopal Church (CME), and so on, what in the name of all that is reasonable would lead one to expect either an effective union presently under COCU or a broader one at a later date? To use a current colloquialism: Let each church group get its own act together first before discussing any more extensive union.

In the Introduction to the study booklet, *The COCU Consensus: In Quest of a Church of Christ Uniting*, editor Moede bewails the fact that "doctrinal disagreement and dispute have been major factors in the division of the Christian Church since early in its history." Moede concludes his first paragraph by asserting that "the effort to find theological agreement among divided churches is of the utmost importance."[26] Why not then start where the differences are presumably the fewest — within separate denominations, not across lines!

In this same booklet, Lewis F. Mudge writes, as the author of the Preface: "With confidence that the Holy Spirit is doing a significant work in our midst, the Theology Commission commends this consensus document to the nine member churches of COCU and to the wider

Christian world."[27] Once again I say, let us leave the Holy Ghost out of the picture. It is presumptuous to use the notion of some supernatural force suddenly bringing to pass agreement where there has been considerable disagreement since early Christian times – and by COCU's own admission. Furthermore, by giving the Holy Ghost the credit for whatever progress Mudge thinks has been achieved through COCU is to threaten the readership with supernatural criticism if anyone should insist that either no progress or progress of the wrong kind has been made. The very word "consensus" in the title of the booklet makes a presumption of far more agreement than exists among the members of the nine churches.

Ecumenism should start at home. If one is committed in conscience to seeing unity among Protestant churches, and one is a member of a church of many parts, say, the United Methodist, the Baptist, the Presbyterian, the United Church of Christ, then one should urge and strive for unity within his/her denomination first. The present non-Episcopal leaders of COCU could act as spearheads for this kind of desperately needed action. Why should not George P. Morgan and Marianne Wolfe work first on behalf of all Presbyterians? Why cannot Vernon Bigler and Howell Wilkins do the same for the Methodists? Why cannot other members of the Drafting Commissions be similarly involved *first and foremost with their own denomination* – presumably the area of their greatest expertise and concern?

By now the reader is aware of some of the reasons why this sort of thing has not been done. Perhaps, the reader also wishes now that something like this *would* be done.

E. Apologia for Denominationalism

At the very grave risk of bucking the trend, of appearing elitist, of being a whiny loser, I should like to suggest that disunity in the Church is not all bad. And this not only for pragmatic reasons but also for cultural and individual reasons which involve the spiritual side of life. I contend as well that no matter what unity has obtained, or will obtain in whatever form, it will never be complete and absolute. And this for reasons of our free will if nothing else.

To those who maintain that even a basic unity founded upon belief in Jesus Christ as Lord of all is enough, to those who add acceptance of Holy Scripture and the two major sacraments, Baptism and Holy Communion, as necessary for sufficiency—to them I would say, you are describing belief, not the Church, for the Church is a corporate body, an organization with an animus of its own. Of those who are fond of invoking the Holy Ghost in matters of union I would ask: Was it not perhaps also the Holy Ghost who produced the divisions to begin with—that is, if you believe your particular denomination holds a larger measure of truth than others?

Few can deny the good that came of the Reformation and the Counter-Reformation. Many would give credit to individual denominations who have had stunning success in the mission fields here and abroad. Most would recognize the fact that, had the divisions not produced separate denominations, many persons would have been lost to the Church. And that has once again become a danger, for the number of lapsed this and that—persons who cannot accept the many violent changes in their own churches and who can not accept a tossed salad of churches either—is increasing day by day.

The average proponent of ecumenism, inexpert as he or she is likely to be in ecclesiastical matters, is so caught up with the elimination of the astonishing divisions within Christianity on a grand scale that the shortcomings of the individual denomination are forgotten. So much ingenuity has been devoted to creating a huge, sweeping administration that advocates of church union fail to see the persistence of difficulties in faith and its grassroots public expression. It is a wonder that any churches have united and remained so for long.

Some churches subscribe to detailed confessions of faith and will not consider any union that does not include the totality of their dogmatic formulations. Other churches may insist upon most of the traditional creedal expressions of the Christian faith, but are flexible on matters not specifically treated in Scripture or the Creeds. Still others are even more flexible and only call for a declaration of belief in Christ as essential.

It is obvious that the first group stands alone. To create a union of churches within the second or third group presents no insurmountable difficulties. But to mix the second and third groups poses enormous problems. For the second group, creeds and dogmas merely exercise certain restrictions in the freedom of one's religious thinking, whereas for the third group such dogmas act as intolerable brakes on personal liberty. Unfortunately, in any consideration of union among Protestant churches, the second and third groups constitute the largest number. Union between such groups is not impossible, but it is very nearly impossible. Hence my urging in the last section to approach union on a large scale through union on a small scale within similar groups. Avoid line-crossing at all costs.

In the case of order we have a threefold division similar to that found in our discussion of faith. There are those churches which, for example, accept only one order of the ministry as divinely ordained and indefectible; they therefore reject other orders and attendant sacraments as invalid. There are other churches which, although they view one form of the ministry as ideal, are willing to admit, if not the actual validity, at least the spiritual reality of other ministries. Still other churches admit the value of order in the church, but are unwilling to pin it down to any one form and are thus able to accept the ministry of any church.

Once again, we see that the first group stands alone. As long as there are churches willing to do so, union within the second or third group is easily accomplished. But when the second and third groups are mixed, it is a different story.

The problem this time is of a different sort. Those in the third group tend to demand of those in the second group that they acknowledge the equality of ministries, something that they cannot do in good conscience. But this attack technique forces the second group, who honestly believes in the validity and propriety of its ministry, to respond timidly and less than honestly, for it feels it must downgrade its own beliefs.

In matters of church union, humility has no place. If people do not speak out honestly and forcefully about what they really believe, there will be no resolution of differences. And the union will not take place. The union will not last either if those tensions, now much more acutely felt after separated units are brought together, are not resolved. *Everyone must state exactly where there are differences and what they are.* Americans are a strange lot. They are known for their friendliness and openness. Yet their conciliatory attitude usually wins over their frankness. In matters of faith leading to any lasting union, only candidness will work.

Other things need to be said. The spirit of competition in America has helped to produce and preserve a plethora of denominations. Without a healthy tension between variations of the faith, religion might have attained a certain sameness, a monotony, which would have led to a deadly lethargy. Truth has been tested, re-examined, and refined. Is it possible that total unity of the

Christian faith might result in such a uniformity that truth could never again be tested? If we look back in time to the Middle Ages when the Church was, to all intents and purposes, one, we discover that the Church was nevertheless wonderfully diverse in thought and action and that its division in the 16th century actually brought on the hardening of opposing positions. It is therefore not a question of union versus denominationalism so much as it is opportunity to express and preserve the riches of individual parts.

EPILOGUE

"A needless Alexandrine ends the song,
And, like a wounded snake,
drags its slow length along."

— *Alexander Pope*

Christian theology is the systemization of doctrines
or beliefs belonging to the Christian way of life. It does
not operate alone but in tension with all the other beliefs
we hold in the modern world. There is also an inner
tension, for its doctrines must cohere internally as well
as externally. It is responsible to itself and to the community which it serves.

Theology is dynamic and without end. It must express the community's beliefs, but it must also be able to
criticize those beliefs. When a conflict arises between
loyalty to community and loyalty to doctrine, then the
community has the choice of accepting the doctrine as it
is or revising it in light of new knowledge.

It is easy to see how theology often comes into
relation with secular beliefs. There has always been an
intellectual connection between theology and philoso-
phy, theology and history, and, in the later history of the
Church, occasionally between theology and the empirical
sciences. In recent years, we have seen connections between theology and psychology, sociology, or even linguistics.

We frequently distinguish between dogmatic theology, which has the task of systematizing various accepted
doctrines, and apologetic theology, which relates those
doctrines to the community. The problems the Church
faces today fall in the column of apologetics. As long as
apologetics is tested against dogmatism, difficulties can

be resolved. It is only when dogma or apologetics alone is relied upon that unrelieved tension is felt.

It is difficult today to achieve a balance between doctrinal prescriptions and intellectual and personal freedom. Insistence upon certain beliefs and behaviors is taken as inhibitory of individual freedoms and the progress of society. An initiatory rite such as Confirmation is viewed as a barrier to be challenged or skirted rather than as the entrance to the privilege of Communion. Canonical and moral qualifications for ordination are seen as outdated impediments to one's inherent "right" to choice of a profession. Membership in a church does not entail the sacrificial giving of money and talent. In a misguided effort to hold on to its members, the Episcopal Church has become secularized and allowed its constituents, lay and clerical alike, to infringe its doctrines. (It is ironic that the Church's strategy to retain members has not worked.) Instead of protecting its people against the disvalues of secularism, the Church has chosen to support many societal objectives in the name of equality, compassion, and personal freedom, when, in fact, none of these is ruled out within a framework of tradition and order.

There is, for example, no good reason why both the 1928 and the 1979 Prayer Book cannot be permitted as service manuals. The freedom allowed would obviously be greater than the restriction to one. The advocates of the 1979 would certainly not insist that other churches of the worldwide Communion use it. The very autonomy of the Episcopal Church gives it the right to allow both books. Different authorized prayer books have never been an impediment to intercommunion.

However, to use autonomy as an argument for permitting the ordination of women in the Episcopal Church is to jeopardize intercommunion within Anglicanism and with other Catholic bodies. This action is of a different and more serious nature than prayer book usage. It is peculiar that the value of uniformity is invoked as a reason for insisting upon only the 1979 Prayer Book, but lack of uniformity of practice is never admitted when discussing female clergy. Who knows but what uniformity in even this issue could have been achieved if progress had been more deliberate, proper, and cooperative?

It is distressing to recall with what vigor and determination the national church went at the matter of prayer book revision; how orders went out to dioceses to examine all material and then to forward it to parishes for their study and reaction. But there were no announcements of a study of female ordination, no booklets prepared, no rationales laid out, no letters from diocesans to their flocks, no sermons, no discussions. A similar situation obtained regarding the consecration of a female bishop: no announcement, no preparation, no study, no sermons, no discussions. Despite our explanations for this cabal, it is amazing there was so little squawking until the deed was accomplished.

In many ways the Church is like a father or a mother—or both parents. It sets standards for its children to follow through the examples of its hierarchy. Most of the time the Church is dependable, predictable, ethical, moral. And even when it sometimes is not, the people are quick to forgive little transgressions.

But what we are witnessing now is something akin to a mid-life crisis. Just as children look in wonder at their aging father who has purchased a little red sportcar, dyed his hair dark, and moved in with a woman half his age, or watch in disbelief as their mother deserts her family and heads off to another city to "do her thing," churchpeople contemplate their church in dismay, for it has lost its stability and all right to serve as parent. Like the real-life people it is supposed to nurture, the Church—that nebulous, hierarchical, administrative body—has fallen prey to the temptations of society, and donned new clothes, found new consorts, and is furiously "doing its thing."

It is time the people took over.

Let the liberals lead the way, for they are the ones who proclaim openness and honesty as the only workable policy. Let them force the bishops to explain cogently why two prayer books cannot co-exist. Let them exact from the bishops an airtight rationale for ordaining women deacons and priests and consecrating them bishops. Let them compel the bishops to show how their policy furthers — not inhibits — union with sister churches of the historic Catholic faith. Let them oblige the bishops to show cause why the Episcopal Church should remain in COCU. Let us leave the Holy Ghost out of it. The Church needs to build a case for itself. The liberals can assist it in doing so.

The traditionalists will not shirk their duty. They will support the liberals in all the steps above; for once, they will join sides with the opposition, for the cause is righteous, and the method is fair and solid.

Simultaneously, the traditionalists must call on the bishops to:

1) *Admit the legality of the 1928 Prayer Book and grant permission to use both the 1928 and 1979 Prayer Book, parish by parish or service by service.* It will be incumbent upon each parish to poll itself on its preference and advise its rector of the results. The rector will then, in keeping with canon law, make the decision for the parish. That decision will be subject to change by the rector and by subsequent rectors.

2) *Announce a moratorium on the ordination of women.* The purpose of the moratorium is to enable the autonomous member churches of the Anglican Communion to consult together and reach a consensus regarding the theological integrity and the advisability from the standpoint of ecumenism of ordaining women. That con-

sensus should then be conveyed to non-Anglican communions for their consideration and comment. The ultimate length of the moratorium should be determined only after preliminary plenary discussion.

3) *Withdraw summarily from COCU.* Just as there is no legal test for membership in COCU, there is no legal prohibition against resigning. If severing all ties seems too abrupt, considering the decades of cooperative involvement, the Episcopal Church can join the Roman Catholic, Lutheran, and Reformed Church in America communions on the COCU Theology Commission. Once the Protestant members of COCU have smoothed out their own differences, and recruited any other like-minded Protestant bodies, the members of the Theology Commission will be able to talk more substantively with them. The Episcopal Church should take no stand on its own, but should be joined by other members of the Anglican Communion after careful consultation with the Roman and the Orthodox Churches.

What if the leadership of the Episcopal Church refuses to accede to these demands?

They will find it very difficult to refuse to listen if the demands originate with the liberal element and are based on the spirit of honesty and openness. These are, after all, their own kind of people. But they *should* listen to anybody — liberal or conservative — for one group is not automatically good or automatically bad, and the bishops' job is to respond to *all* their flock.

But what if they still refuse to listen? Maybe their personal agendas are so compelling that they hear no voices but their own!

The people must ask again and wait patiently for compliance. They can explain to the bishops — if it is not obvious — that no harm will be done if they take the recommended measures. Everything is temporary; the church can always revert to the position it now assumes.

Nothing is lost. There is no hurry. And, they might ask, should we not do everything we can to avoid schism?

But what if the leadership is still hard of hearing?

Then the people must protest. And *that* the bishops will surely understand, for that is exactly how women achieved ordination! Part of the protest will have to involve withholding money from the parish, the diocese, and the national church. That move will get everybody's attention. So will schism.

Of course, this process should not have to go beyond step one. Bishops are, after all, the chief pastors and should have the best for all their people in mind. They would naturally want to hear all aspects of an issue, for it is their business to tread extremely carefully where the historic faith is concerned. Why is there anything to fear?

There is plenty to fear because the bishops of the Episcopal Church have a dubious track record. The mere fact that they exercised no effort at the parish level to discuss the issue of female ordination in advance of implementation indicates an unwillingness — in spite of their avowed liberal stance — to be thoroughly open. Their investment in COCU is such that they think they will suffer embarrassment if they have to withdraw even if only for a brief time. They will probably have to be pressured to comply.

A sad day has dawned for the Episcopal Church. The one unified non-Roman church is splitting itself apart in the hope of drawing together incredibly disparate elements of Protestantism and American secular society. And to what end? To the Episcopal Church's dissolution and disappearance. No longer can its people look to it for predictability and stability. No longer can outsiders aspire to belong to something that is sure.

Where lies the hope?

The hope lies in the Church's true liberalism: its willingness to open its mind and its heart and accept, as was its custom, diversity within structure. Maybe then the Holy Ghost can return as the true conservator.

Amen.

- NOTES -

1. Robert C. Harvey, *A House Divided* (Winchester, NH: The Canterbury Guild, 1976), 14.

2. Ibid.

3. Ibid., 14-15.

4. Malcolm Muggeridge, "The Great Liberal Death Wish," edited by Ian Hunter, *Things Past* (New York: Morrow 1979), 220-221.

5. Michael Oakeshott, "On Being Conservative," *Rationalism in Politics and Other Essays* (New York: Methuen, 1962), 170.

6. William A. Thompson. Executive Director. Church Deployment Office, Episcopal Church Center, New York, letter dated May 29, 1990.

7. Edwin G. Wappler, "Anglicans and the New Morality," *The Anglican Moral Choice* (Wilton, CT: Morehouse-Barlow, 1983), 23.

8. Marion J. Hatchett. *Commentary on the American Prayer Book* (New York: Seabury Press, 1980), 13.

9. Ibid., 266.

10. Jill Robson, "Women's Images of God and Prayer," *The Way*, Apr. 1986, vol. 26, no. 2, 91-103.

11. Gail Ramshaw-Schmidt. "An Inclusive Language Lectionary," *Worship*, 1984, 58:31, 35-36.

12. Donald G. Bloesch, *The Battle for the Trinity* (Ann Arbor: Vine Books, 1985), 21.

13. Herbert Schlossberg, *Idols for Destruction* (Nashville: Thomas Nelson Publishers, 1983), 235.

14. Ibid.

15. S. Mark Heim, "Gender and Creed: Confessing a Common Faith," *The Christian Century*, vol. 102, 1985, 13:381.

16. Ibid.. 380.

17. *Insight*, Apr. 24, 1989.

18. Frank S. Mead, *Handbook of Denominations* (Nashville, New York: Abingdon Press, 1970), 5th ed., 96.

19. *Episcopal Church Annual*, 1989, 18-19.

20. Ibid.

21. *Yearbook of American and Canadian Churches*, edited by Constant H. Jacquet, Jr. (Nashville: Abingdon Press, 1989).

22. Eugene Peterson, "How Pure Must a Pastor Be?" *Leadership*, Spring 1988.

23. Mark B. Thompson, "Who Should Be Ordained?" *The Living Church*, Jul. 21, 1985, 10.

24. Edmond L. Browning, *Forward Day by Day*, Forward Movement Publications (Cincinnati: General Convention of the Episcopal Church), Nov. 1989-Jan. 1990, 67.

25. Indifferentism is what one might call systematic in-
    difference to religion: that is, the belief that all reli-
    gions have equal validity.

26. Gerald F. Moede, editor, *The COCU Consensus: In
    Quest of a Church of Christ Uniting*, 1985.

27. Ibid.

- INDEX -

A

Aberdeen, Cathedral of, 101

Act of Supremacy, 84

Act of Uniformity, 90

Affirmation of St. Louis, x

analogies, 36

Augustine, St., 82

Anselm, St., 25

Apostolicae Curae, 41

Apostolic Succession, 8, 9, 71, 79, 101, 103, 107, 108, 145

Aquinas, St. Thomas, 36

Arianism, 88

Aristotelianism, 64

Association of Theological Schools, 48

Assumption of the BVM, 67

B

Bakker, Jim, 55

Barth, Karl, 36

Blair, James, 98, 99

Blake, the Rev. Eugene Carson, 15

Blessed Virgin Mary (BVM), 39, 67, 70

Bloesch. Donald G., 36

Boleyn, Anne, 84

Brent, Bp. Charles H., 137

Browning, Bp. Edmond L., 128, 131

Bryan, William Jennings, 54

C

Calvin, John, 77

Cerularius, Michael, 73

Charlemagne, 72

Charles, Otis, 48

Charles II, 99

Charles V, 84

Chicago-Lambeth Quadrilateral, 7-9, 24, 128

"Church" and "churches" (definition), 7

Church Congress, x

Church Deployment Office, xvi

Church of South India (CSI), 91, 92

Compton, Bp. Henry, 98

COCU, iv, 14-19, 52, 62, 106, 108, 127, 128, 135, 152, 153, 161, 163

Constantine, 71, 114

Continuing Church Movement, 128

Cranmer, Archblshop Thomas, 21, 84, 86, 90, 142

creeds: See primarily Chap. V, C. Faith

D

Darby, John Nelson, 53

Darrow, Clarence, 54

deaconesses, 47

Diet of Speyer, 68

dispensationalism, 53

Dix, Dom Gregory, 42, 91

E

Episcopal Church Publishing Co. (ECPC), 45

Episcopal Divinity School, 48

Episcopal Life, iv

Episcopal Synod of America, x, 128, 133, 134, 135, 149

Erasmus, Desiderius, 77, 144

Evangelical and Catholic Mission (ECM), 128, 133

F

Faith and Order Movement, 136

Falwell, Jerry, 55

Federal Council of Churches of Christ in America, 137

Fellowship of Concerned Churchmen, x

filioque clause, 73

Foreign Missions Conference of North America, 136

G

Galileo, 5

Gavin, Franklin Stanton Burns, 75

grace, 70

Graham, Billy, 55, 56

Great Schism (of the East), 73

Griffith, the Rev. David, 102

H

Harris. Bp. Barbara C., iv, xviii, 29, 45, 46, 149

Harvey, Bp. Robert C., vii

Hatchett, Marion J., 22

Heim, S. Mark, 39, 40

Hines, Bp. John E., vii

Hunt, the Rev. Robert, 96

Huntington, the Rev. William Reed, 7

Huss, Jan, 76

Hutten, Ulrich von, 77

I

iconostasis, 75
Ignatius, Bp. of Syria, 11, 64
Ignatius (of Antiock), 64
Ignatius (of Constantinople), 72-73
Immaculate Conception, 67
inclusive language, 29-34
indifferentism, 140
indulgences, 77, 78, 83
intercession, 70
Internal Revenue Service, vii
International Council on English Texts (ICET), 23

J

Jahweh, 39
James I, 96
James II, 97
Jamestown, Va., 95, 96, 97
Jewel, Bp. of Salisbury, 82
Jones, Bob, 55
Judaism, 64

K

Katherine of Aragon, 84
Keble, the Rev. John, 103, 104

L

Lambeth Conference, iv, 89
Laws, Curtis Lee, 54
Leaming, the Rev. Jeremiah, 101
Leipzig Disputation, 145
Leonard, Bp. Graham, 135

liberal (definition), ix

literalism, 54

London Co., 96

Luther, Martin, 69, 77-79, 84, 144, 145

M

Manning, the Rev. Henry Edward, 104

Mather, Increase, 99

McIntire, Carl, 55

Melanchthon, Philip, 77

merit, 70

metaphors, 36

Muggeridge, Malcolm, ix

Muhlenberg, the Rev. Willlam Augustus, 47

N

Nashotah House, 116

National Council of Churches, 30, 48

New Zealand, iv

Newman, the Rev. John Henry, 103, 104

Nida, Eugene A., 37

P

Paisley, the Rev. Ian, 141, 142

papal infallibility, 66, 71, 144

Papalists, 90

Patrick, St., 82

Peale, the Rev. Norman Vincent, 56

Pentecostals, 55

Peter, St., 65

"Philadelphia Eleven," 44

Photius, 72-73

Platonism, 64

pluralism, 139

Politzer, the Rev. Jerome F., 23, 24, 26

Pope, Bp. Clarence, 133

Popes:

Potter, Bp. Alonzo, 47

Prayer Book(s), iii, viii, xiii, 2, 20-29, 47, 88, 90, 91, 92, 94, 103, 107, 108, 126, 132, 148, 159, 160, 161

Prayer Book Society, xiv, 23, 51, 123, 128

Prohibition, 4

Provoost, Bp. Samuel, 102

purgatory, 67, 70

Puritans, 90, 99, 100

Pusey, the Rev. Edward Bouverie, 103, 104

Swaggart, Jimmy, 55
Swedish Lutheran Church, 3
synagogue, 11

T

Temple, Archbishop William, 48
Thirty-nine Articles, 88
Tractarians, 103, 105
traditionalist (definitlon), x
Tridentine Mass, 93

U

United Methodist Church, 3

V

Valla, Lorenzo, 77
veneration of saints, 70

W

Wantland, Bp. William, 133
Watchman-Examiner, The, 54
White, Bp. William, 101-102
William and Mary, 97
Witness, The, 46
Wittenberg, 77-78
Wyclif, John, 76
World Council of Churches, iv

Z

Zwingli, Ulrich, 77